ENCYCLOPEDIA OF THE
Animal World

Vol 19   Stargazers – Titis

Bay Books Sydney

1075

Astropecten aurantiacus, a starfish that burrows in the sand. The entry on starfish starts on p. 1726.

STARGAZERS, two families containing bottom-living perch-like fishes, the eyes of which are set on top of the head, the fish appearing to stare upwards, hence the common name. The principal difference between these two families is that the uranoscopids have electric organs. They are marine fishes found in all tropical and temperate waters, from the shallows to the depths. They have stocky, depressed bodies, large heads and a mouth that is directed upwards. The European stargazer *Uranoscopus scaber* is common in the Mediterranean. It grows to 1 ft (30 cm) long and has little flaps of tissue inside the mouth that resemble small worms. These appear to act as lures, enticing fishes inside the mouth.

The electric organs are formed from muscles and are lodged in pits behind the eyes. Although small, the discharge from these organs reaches 50 volts. It is thought to be partly a means of defence and partly a means of stunning small fishes. Stargazers also defend themselves by means of poisonous spines above the pectoral fins. The spines are grooved and there is a poison gland at their base, the poison running along the groove and into the wound. It has been known to be fatal to humans. These fishes are extremely difficult to see, even when in shallow water, because they bury themselves in the sand with only the eyes and tip of snout showing. In some species the nostrils open into the mouth so that a stream of sediment-free water can be drawn in.

One of the best known of the dactyloscopids is *Dactyloscopus tridigitatus*. It is found in the warmer parts of the Atlantic. FAMILIES: Uranoscopidae, Dactyloscopidae, ORDER: Perciformes, CLASS: Pisces.

STARLINGS, a family of 105 species of medium-sized to large songbirds having, in general, slender bills, a rather upright stance and smooth, often glossy, plumage. They occur naturally in the Old World only, but a few species have been introduced into other parts of the world, where they have usually proved to be pests.

The typical starlings have slender, straight and tapering bills, and when feeding in turf, among plants or leaves, they thrust the closed bill into the ground or vegetation and open it, making a hole. The eyes are set close to the base of the bill and the bird looks along the opened bill, down into the hole, and seizes any food which the probing has revealed. These close-set eyes give the starlings their characteristic appearance. Starlings of the genus *Sturnus* have elongated spiky feathers on the head and throat and are soberly coloured in black-grey, white, buff and, more rarely pale pink, with some iridescence on the darker plumage. They are mainly terrestrial in their feeding, and walk and run with ease. Their flight is rapid and direct, with constant beating of the tapered wings. The relatively similar proportions during flight of the tapering wings, tapering head and bill, and short tail, gives these birds the 'star'-like outline which accounts for their original name. Outside the breeding season they tend to flock together for feeding and roosting. Some of the roost-flocks are of huge size and the rapid co-ordinated manoeuvring of such flocks over the roost is typical of starling behaviour. At times the numbers may be such that the weight of the birds breaks the branches and the accumulated droppings kill trees in plantations where they roost. They have taken to flying into the centres of many cities to roost on the ledges of buildings.

The food of starlings consists of insects and invertebrates, fruits, some seeds and parts of green plants. The typical probing starlings specialize on insect foods to a greater extent than do some of the others. They will also take ripe fruit, however, and may do so to an extent that makes them unpopular with fruit-growers.

The Common starling *Sturnus vulgaris* has been introduced into North America and eastern Australia and has established itself and spread on both continents. The Rosy pastor *S. roseus* is a bird of the Asiatic steppes and like other species of those parts may periodically show large increases in numbers, and then in an unfavourable period spread out over wide areas, at such times often appearing in western Europe. The Asiatic *mynahs, small brown or grey species of the genus *Acridotheres* or the larger glossy-plumaged *Gracula* species, are more stoutly built and have the shorter heavier bills of more generalized feeders. They tend to have bristly or crested foreheads, bare skin around the eyes, and yellow wattles on the sides of the head. An African species, the Wattled starling *Creatophora carunculata* shows this development of head wattles to a much greater extent. In the breeding season the male loses the head feathers and has a bald grey head and long pendant black wattles hanging well below the throat. This species follows the locust swarms in large flocks to feed on them. Breeding occurs where the female locusts stop to lay their eggs, the hatching insects being used as food for the young starlings.

Some of the more heavily-built, mynah-like starlings are isolated on islands in the East Indies and Pacific regions where they have developed distinct forms. They show two trends: the elaboration or the loss of crests. The Crested starling *Basilornis galeatus* of Sula has a glossy purplish plumage with yellow and white shoulder patches, and has developed a fine large crest shaped as a laterally flattened fan. At the other extreme Dumont's mynah *Mino*

dumontii of New Guinea has the feathering reduced and rough orange skin around the eyes spreading to occupy much of the head, while in the Philippine coleto *Sarcops calva* the head is bald. Rothschild's mynah *Leucopsar rothschildi* of Bali has a white plumage, with bright blue bare skin around the eyes, and a fine spiky erectile crest. Several large starlings, one at least having a fan-shaped crest, were present on the Mascarene Islands of the Indian Ocean when these were first discovered by Europeans, but have now become extinct.

The Glossy starlings are the most brightly coloured group within the family. Their plumage is sleek and shiny, often with a rather oily sheen, and is coloured in strong iridescent blues, purples and greens. The Amethyst starling *Cinnyricinclus leucogaster* is most striking; for, in contrast with a dull, brown-streaked female, the male is vivid magenta purple over head, back, wings and tail, and white below. This purple gloss shows bluish in some lights. In this species, and a number of others, there is a contrasting bright yellow iris to the eye. In several species the underside shows contrasting colour, the vivid blue and green of the back being set off by chestnut-red in *Spreo* species, and by bright yellow in the Golden-breasted starling *Lamprotornis regius*.

A related group, the Red-winged starlings *Onychognathus* species, occur in Africa. They are larger, long-tailed birds, usually dark and glossy, with a greyish-streaked head in the female, and, in both sexes, chestnut-red on the primary feathers which are only conspicuous in flight. They are more frequently found near rocky places, such as ravines or cliffs. One species has a bristly crest on the forehead over the bill.

One of the odder starlings is the Celebes starling *Scissirostrum dubium*, which has a rather stout, deep bill, apparently adapted for chiselling. It feeds, however, on fruit, and appears to use the bill only for excavating its nest hole in dead wood, clinging woodpecker-fashion in order to do so. The most specialized group of the family are the *oxpeckers, two species of the genus *Buphagus*, that are adapted to clambering over the bodies of large grazing animals feeding on ticks. They are dull-coloured with red or yellow bills; and are sufficiently different to be placed as a separate subfamily.

None of the starlings has a really musical voice, and calls and songs are usually a mixture of squeaky, whistled and bubbling notes; occasionally fairly melodious but often harsh or piercingly shrill. Some species are natural mimics. Among the medley of odd

Common European starling, an adaptable and successful species that has been introduced into North America and Australia.

Opposite: a starfish, righting itself after having been turned upside-down. See starfish p. 1726.

Superb Glossy starling *Spreo superbus* of East Africa.

STEINBOK *Raphicerus campestris,* a small gazelle from South and East Africa. See Dwarf antelopes.

STEM-REPTILES, a name sometimes used for the extinct reptiles of the order Cotylosauria because they are the most primitive reptiles known and represent the basal stock from which all other reptiles have descended. They flourished during the Carboniferous and Permian periods, 300–225 million years ago. See reptiles.

STENTOR, an extremely large ciliate protozoan which reaches a length of $\frac{1}{12}$ in (2 mm). Most species are also quite colourful. The end of the ciliate bearing the mouth is very much expanded and the opposite end is narrower, giving the whole animal the appearance of a trumpet. The macronucleus is very large and has the form of a string of sausages. *Stentor coerulus* is common in ponds and is a striking protozoan, green in colour and striped in wide bands that run the length of the animal. When feeding *Stentor* attaches to the substratum by its narrow end. It divides asexually by a division across the body and a new mouth grows at the constriction which forms when the ciliate divides. It also reproduces sexually by conjugation, which is typical of ciliates in general. It does not apparently form cysts. The importance of *Stentor* lies in its large size and the fact that it provides a very useful model for studies on ciliary movement. By microsurgical techniques it is possible to isolate specific regions of the ring of cilia surrounding the mouth and studies such as

Stentor coerulus, one of the largest living protozoans, grows up to 2 mm in length. This ciliate feeds on bacteria, small algae and rotifers which are wafted towards the buccal funnel leading to the cytostome by the ring of adoral membranelles.

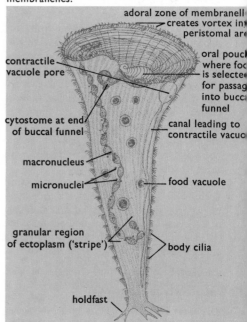

noises that passes for song in the Common starling there may be imitations of other birds, animals and even mechanically-produced sounds. This species can occasionally be taught to imitate human speech, but the Hill mynahs *Gracula* when taken young and reared, are superb mimics and may learn extensive repertoires.

Starling nests tend to be rather crudely made and bulky. Those built in the open in trees are usually rounded structures with a side-entrance, rarely a cup; but when a natural hole is used a cup-shaped nest may be built within. Some African species, such as *Spreo superbus,* may use old nests of the larger weaver species. The Common starling, using a hole in a tree or house, may also retain this as a year-round roost and with successive nestings may accumulate a very considerable amount of material. This species occasionally nests in thick creepers or shrubs on the walls of houses. The switch from natural holes in trees or rocks to holes in buildings has been made by several species; and the erection of buildings in places where natural cavities are scarce may aid the spread of these birds. The Bank mynah *Acridotheres ginginianus* may make its own burrow in the miniature cliff of a river bank. Most starlings make solitary nests, although in some species they may be near to each other in a loose colony. In the

genus *Aplonis,* dull greenish Glossy starlings, of the Oriental and Australasian regions, pairs of some species may nest in very close proximity, a number occupying a single large mass of epiphytic plants on a tree; and one species, the Colonial starling *Aplonis metallica* builds colonial pendant nests in trees.

Starling eggs are most often uniform light blue, in some species sparsely marked with red spots or streaks. Spreo starlings have eggs which, when freshly laid, are deep green, but this is due to a yellow pigment combined with the blue colour. The yellow pigment gradually fades, and if the eggs are kept, even if shut away from the light, they become blue like the rest in about a year. FAMILY: Sturnidae, ORDER: Passeriformes, CLASS: Aves.

STEELHEAD *Salmo gairdneri,* a North American trout that migrates from the sea into rivers to spawn. The name steelhead is used in the United States for this migratory form and at one time it was thought to be distinct from the non-migratory Rainbow trout (formerly known as *S. irideus*). It is now known that the two belong to the same species, *S. gairdneri,* in much the same way that the Sea trout is merely the migratory form of the Brown trout *S. trutta.* FAMILY: Salmonidae, ORDER: Salmoniformes, CLASS: Pisces.

these have shown that the movement of a cilium is triggered off by the movement of the one in front of it. The possibility of a fibrillar system—fibrillae are minute threads—co-ordinating the movement of the cilia seems unlikely. SUBCLASS: Spirotricha, ORDER: Heterotrichida, CLASS: Ciliata, PHYLUM: Protozoa.   F.E.G.C.

STICK INSECTS, often called walking sticks in America, get their name from the shape of the body which is very long and slender, and usually green or brown so that they look like slender twigs. The deception is enhanced by the fact that if they are disturbed they remain quite motionless. With too much disturbance they fall to the ground without showing any sign of life, with the long thin legs held close against the body so that they look just like twigs amongst the litter of leaves under plants. The largest Stick insects may be up to 9 in (23 cm) long, but the species commonly kept in schools and laboratories, *Carausius morosus,* is not more than about 4 in (10 cm) long at most.

Stick insects are usually without wings even as adults and even in those species which have wings the forewings are usually very small. Since the forewings offer so little protection, the front edges of the hindwings are leathery and cover the membranous parts of the wings when they are folded up. Stick insect eggs are hard and rounded about an $\frac{1}{8}$ in (3 mm) across. They drop to the ground as they are being laid and often remain for a long time before hatching. The young, when they hatch, are about $\frac{1}{2}$ in (12·5 mm) long, but otherwise resemble the adults. They feed on leaves and in Australia, where Stick insects are particularly abundant, they may completely defoliate eucalyptus trees and so are of some economic importance.

Above: Stick insect *Carausius morosus* hatching. This species is often kept in insectaria and breeds parthenogenetically: males are very seldom found. From the unfertilized eggs, which resemble seeds (2 mm), after some months, the young insects (10 mm!) emerge, by lifting a small lid. The empty egg-shell is often carried about for several days after birth. Stick insects can regenerate lost legs.

New Zealand Smooth stick insect *Clitarchus hookeri* is, by its shape and colour as well as its habit of remaining still, deceptively like a twig.

Like the Leaf insect, which belongs to the same order, Stick insects are mainly found in the tropics, but *Carausius morosus* is kept in laboratories in many parts of the world. This species and some others are remarkable in that males are very rare indeed. The females lay eggs which are not fertilized and these eggs produce only females. This phenomenon of development from unfertilized eggs is known as *parthenogenesis.

Another odd thing about Stick insects is that if a young one is caught by a leg it can escape by simply breaking off the leg. For a time it hobbles about on five legs, but a new leg develops during the course of subsequent moults so the insect is restored to its normal condition. The deliberate breaking off of an appendage in this way is called *autotomy. Lizards show the same phenomenon when they shed their tails. ORDER: Phasmida, CLASS: Insecta, PHYLUM: Arthropoda. R.F.C.

STICKLEBACKS, a family of very common freshwater and marine fishes of the northern hemisphere, characterized by the series of sharp spines in front of the soft-rayed dorsal fin. The Three-spined stickleback *Gasterosteus aculeatus* is found in almost every brook and pond in England and is common throughout Europe, across Asia to Japan and in North America. There are, as the name suggests, three spines before the

Male stickleback.

soft dorsal fin and the pelvic fins are each reduced to a single spine. It was formerly thought that there were several species of sticklebacks with three spines, but Professor Léon Bertin finally showed that there is a single but variable species. Thus populations from northern waters and in the sea produce larger individuals which have a series of bony plates or scutes along the flanks. Those from the south are smaller and the scutes are reduced to about two at the front of the body. The species reaches a maximum of about 4 in (10 cm) in length.

In spring, the male Three-spined stickleback changes to a bright blue with red on the chest. He then constructs a nest from plant strands which are stuck together with a sticky secretion from the kidneys. The nest is ball-like and the male enters it and makes a large central chamber. The nest may be placed in a hollow on the bottom but nests have also been found in old tins lying in the water. The male defends the nest from other males or from intruders but entices gravid females to enter and deposit their eggs. After the eggs are fertilized, the male guards the nest and aerates the eggs by fanning movements with the pectoral fins, carefully removing any dead or infertile eggs.

Sticklebacks are extremely voracious and probably rival the bluefish, although on a much smaller scale. A naturalist of the 18th

century once observed that one of his sticklebacks consumed 74 young dace of $\frac{1}{4}$ in (6 mm) long and two days later ate a further 62 dace and was presumed to have been capable of taking more. These fishes are easy to keep in captivity provided that live food is given. The life span appears to be three or four years. Although essentially a freshwater species, some live in rock pools and a few have been caught several miles out to sea.

Two other species are found in Europe and Asia. The Ten-spined stickleback *Pungitius pungitius* is less common in England than the previous species and is often found in brackish water. It is, however, widespread across Europe and occurs in North America. Other species of *Pungitius* are found in Asia. The marine Fifteen-spined stickleback *Spinachia spinachia* grows to about 9 in (23 cm) in length and is commonly found around European coasts. It is more elongated than the freshwater species and leads a solitary life amongst weeds. It has a brown, well camouflaged body and also constructs a nest.

In North America there are two species of sticklebacks, the Four-spined stickleback *Apeltes quadracus* and the American brook stickleback *Culea inconstans,* which usually has five spines and is the more northerly of the two. The latter species may have four or six spines but more usually five. Some variation also occurs in the other species, the Three-spined occasionally having two or four spines and the Fifteen-spined sometimes having fourteen or sixteen.

Although the sticklebacks are common fishes that have been studied since the beginnings of modern ichthyology in the 16th century, they still present rather a puzzle. They have long been linked with the Sea horses and pipefishes, but this relationship seems questionable. The only fossils found have been very similar to the modern forms so that their nearest relatives, apart from the tubemouths, are still in doubt. FAMILY: Gasterosteidae, ORDER: Gasterosteiformes, CLASS: Pisces.

STICKLEBACK MANURE. In bygone days, before rivers became polluted, Three-spined sticklebacks sometimes appeared in vast shoals. There is an 18th century record of a man being employed to scoop out these fish for use as manure on the fields. He was paid one penny for 2 bushels and could earn 4 shillings a day, which represents a catch of over 750 gallons (3,400 lt) of fish. Considering the small size of the stickleback this is a phenomenal number of fish and, considering the voracity of the stickleback, it gives some idea of the productivity of the once-unpolluted rivers.

STILT BUGS, small fragile insects with long thin legs. They can be found in grasslands in tropical and temperate regions although they are never very common and have not been much studied. FAMILY: Berytidae, SUBORDER: Heteroptera, ORDER: Hemiptera, CLASS: Insecta, PHYLUM: Arthropoda.

STILTS, very long-legged wading birds which, with *avocets, form the family Recurvirostridae. They are distinguished by their legs which are longer in proportion to body-size than in any other wader and by their small heads and thin, dark, almost straight bills (in contrast to the upcurved bills of the avocets). Their plumage is chiefly black and white, but the Banded stilt *Cladorhynchus leucocephala* also has a chestnut breastband. The latter is confined to Australia while the stilt *Himantopus himantopus* has a world-wide distribution, five geographical races having been named by different qualifying adjectives describing the plumage, for example the Black-winged stilt of the southern Palearctic. They are catholic in choice of habitat, feeding in both salt and freshwater lagoons and flooded grassland. The Banded stilt breeds beside temporary salt lakes, feeding on the shrimps found there. FAMILY : Recurvirostridae, ORDER: Charadriiformes, CLASS: Aves.

STIMULUS, a signal from the environment which is received by an animal's sense organ. Stimuli may be physical (e.g. light, heat, sound, or mechanical) or chemical. They come from the animal's surroundings, both the inanimate and the animate. It is by them that an animal gains information about the warmth of the air, the colour of another animal's feathers, the movements of a predator which may destroy it or the smell of its own lair.

Stimuli are forms of energy: light energy, heat energy, the energy of sound and probably chemical energy in the substances which are smelled or tasted. The energy in the stimulus is converted by the sense organ into impulses which travel along nerves to the central nervous system. Thus, the energy of a sound wave sets the ear-drum of a mammal vibrating, this in turn agitates the chain of bones across the middle ear which make contact with the inner ear. The vibrations travel into the fluid of the inner ear, causing the Reissner's membrane to move up and down stimulating the receptor cells of the ear. As a result some of the many cells send impulses to the brain, which can interpret them as sounds of a certain loudness, pitch etc.

Sense organs act as transducers for they transform the energy of the stimulus into the electrical energy of the nerve impulse, just as a microphone converts sound waves into electrical charges in a wire. Stimuli represent

The stingray is fairly common in shallow waters, especially in summer, off the coasts of Europe.

actual objects in the surroundings and so they carry information about the surroundings. This information is turned into a code of nerve impulses by the sense organ. It is this set of impulses which goes to the brain, not the heat or the light or the sound of the stimulus.

Stimuli are often complex. Most objects, particularly other living things, produce stimuli of a number of different kinds. Vision alone may come from stimuli representing colour, shape, movement and brightness but often added to this is sound and perhaps smell. All this information in its coded form has to be sorted out by the nervous system. But certain elements in a complex stimulus may have more significance than others. Social signals are produced by one member of a species and cause, or release, certain behaviour in another member of the same species. These are called 'releasers'. They can be distinguished from the stimuli which come from other parts of the environment which can be called 'sign stimuli'. The colour-pattern of a flower that attracts a bee to it is a sign stimulus.

When releasers are analyzed it is found that an animal responds to parts only of the whole stimulus. Thus, a male stickleback will court a dummy female fish which is a poor representation of a real fish provided that it has a swollen abdomen. Indeed, after a real female fish has deposited its eggs, and its abdomen has gone back to its normal size, the male's response changes from courtship to aggression and it drives the female away

from the eggs. Similarly, it will attack a crudely-made model of a male fish provided that it has a red underside—the courtship livery of the male stickleback.

Not all of the sorting of stimuli takes place within the central nervous system, a certain amount of information is filtered by the sense organ itself. In the optic lobe of an octopus, for example, there are cells connected to arrays of retinal cells in the eye, which fire off impulses into the brain more strongly when certain simple patterns fall on those particular cells. Some respond to horizontal shapes and others to vertical, for instance. In this way the shape of an object is crudely analyzed before nerve impulses reach the brain at all.   J.D.C.

STINGRAYS, a family of ray-like fishes with a venomous spine at the base of the tail capable of inflicting a painful or even fatal wound. The greatly flattened body and wing-like pectoral fins vary in outline from round to triangular or diamond-shaped followed by a thin and whip-like tail that may be longer than the body. The eyes are on top of the head and close behind are the spiracles through which water is drawn to aerate the gills, the latter being on the underside behind the mouth. On the upper side and near to the base of the tail (not at its tip, as is commonly thought) is the sting, a sharp spine with a pair of grooves down the hind edges in which lie the glandular cells that secrete the venom. The spine, which is usually 3–4 in (7·5–10 cm) long but may be up to 15 in (38 cm) in a large fish, is sometimes followed by one to four additional spines. The sting is used solely in defence, the fish lashing the tail from side to side or up and down, sometimes with sufficient force to drive the spine deep into a plank or through a limb. There are about 90 species of stingray, ranging in size from less than 1 ft (30 cm) across the disc of the body to 6–7 ft (1·8–2·1 m) in the case of Captain Cook's stingaree *Dasyatis brevicaudata* of Australasian waters and *D. centroura* of the western North Atlantic. A common species off the Atlantic shores of Europe and in the Mediterranean is the stingray *D. pastinaca,* a species that was well known to Pliny, who repeated the fable that the sting would wither a tree if driven into the trunk. Stingrays lie on the bottom and are often extremely well camouflaged, so that great care should be taken when wading on sandy or muddy beaches where these fishes are known to occur. Some 1,500 accidents with stingrays are reported in the United States every year, mostly of a minor, but nonetheless very painful nature, although some fatalities have been recorded when the sting has penetrated the abdomen causing paralysis of the muscles of the heart. In many parts of the world the spines are used as tips for native spears. The stingrays are bottom-living fishes that feed on shellfish, crustaceans and fishes, the food being crushed or ground up by a pavement of teeth in the jaws. All species are ovoviviparous, the young hatching within the uterus of the female and only later being born.

Members of the genus *Potamotrygon* are found in freshwaters in South America, where they are greatly feared by the local fishermen. The Butterfly rays, often placed in a separate family Gymnuridae, have very short tails, in some species without a sting. The Lesser butterfly ray *Gymnura micrura* is fairly abundant along part of the American Atlantic coast and grows to a width of about 3 or 4 ft (about 1 m), but the rather rare Atlantic coast Giant butterfly ray *G. altavela* reaches 12 ft (3·6 m) from the tip of one pectoral 'wing' to the other. The Butterfly rays are highly coloured, with lace-like markings of browns, greens and purples.

The Round stingrays (family Urolophidae) are circular in outline and have short and stubby tails, again armed with a sting. The Round stingray *Urolophus jamaicensis* of the western North Atlantic is very common in Jamaican waters and is particularly dreaded by the fishermen. FAMILY: Dasyatidae, ORDER: Hypotremata, CLASS: Chondrichthyes.

STINKBUG, North American name for bugs of the large family Pentatomidae. The pentatomids, in common with many other bugs, possess glands secreting substances which are pungent smelling or definitely obnoxious in some species. The English name, *Shield bug which is applied to the Pentatomidae and to a few other closely allied families, seems a more generally applicable name for the group. The pentatomids are moderately large bugs having flattened, shield-shaped bodies which are often brightly and distinctly patterned. One of the dorsal plates of the middle segment (metathorax) of the thorax is enlarged to form a prominent triangular shield which may cover much of the wings. The pentatomids occur in all the continents except Antarctica, but are especially common in Africa, South America and the Indo-Australian region.

Most species of pentatomids lay eggs in masses on various plants and their larvae (also known as nymphs) resemble the adults except they are wingless and are often differently coloured. Some female pentatomids, for example the Birch shield bug *Elasmucha grisea,* guard their eggs and young larvae by covering them with their body until they are fully active. The great majority of the family are plant feeders but a few species are either entirely predatory on other insects or may feed on both plants and animals. Most pentatomids are of little economic importance but some are serious pests of cotton, cabbage, tomato and fruit trees. One of the most important is the Harlequin bug *Murgantia histrionica,* which is exceedingly destructive to cabbage and related plants in the southern United States. FAMILY: Pentatomidae, SUBORDER: Heteroptera, ORDER: Hemiptera, CLASS: Insecta, PHYLUM: Arthropoda. M.J.P.

STINKPOT, a widely used vernacular name for the common Musk turtle *Sternotherus odoratus* of North America. Extremely abundant, it is the only Musk turtle to occur over most of the eastern half of the United States. Adults seldom measure more than 4 in (10 cm) in length and are dun coloured, but the tiny hatchlings have brighter markings, especially on the plastron. The term 'stinkpot' derives from the animal's habit of voiding a vile smelling anal secretion when picked up or otherwise threatened. This habit is soon lost in captivity and the species makes a hardy, interesting pet. FAMILY: Kinosternidae, ORDER: Testudines, CLASS: Reptilia.

STOAT, or ermine *Mustela erminea,* a small carnivore closely related to the weasel but slightly larger and readily distinguishable by the longer tail with the characteristic black tip. Although the sexes are of similar appearance there is a striking size difference: while the male may measure 17·3 in (44 cm) and weigh 15·5 oz (445 gm), the female is rarely over 10·2 in (26 cm) long and may weigh less than 6 oz (170 gm). Confusingly a small female stoat may be the same size as a large male weasel but the tuft of black hair on the tail immediately identifies the stoat. The back is brown or russet and the underside white or cream coloured with an even line separating the two.

It has a north-temperate range encompassing the forest and tundra zones of Eurasia and North America. In the northern parts of this range, ermines usually take on an overall white colour in winter, after moulting, save for the black tail tip. The ventral surface will often be much yellower than the dorsal, due to the secretions from the anal glands used to mark territorial boundaries. This change in pelage colour can be induced experimentally at any time of the year by lowering the temperature and shortening the number of daylight hours and it would appear that these are the two triggering factors concerned. The stoat lives in woods, hedges, or wherever undergrowth is thick enough to provide sufficient cover. Mainly terrestrial, it may climb and swim when hunting. Stoats rarely come out into the open, preferring to skirt a field or a clearing rather than risk falling prey to a kite or a buzzard while crossing it.

These small carnivores feed mostly on voles and mice but large insects, earthworms, shrews and moles may also be eaten. Young rabbits are only occasionally killed by stoats. Standing motionless on its hindlegs, neck arched, the stoat hunting alone will sight its prey and then chase after it with surprising speed and agility. An unerringly accurate neck bite swiftly kills the victim which may be left on the spot or dragged back to the den. Often crepuscular, even diurnal in certain places, the stoat can be seen disappearing under a bush or racing across the road with the typical mustelid humped-back gallop.

Mating takes place in June followed by delayed implantation which retards the birth until the following spring. The blastocyst does not become implanted in the uterine wall until a month before parturition. The young may be born in a hollow log or under a rock pile. The cubs open their eyes 9 to 12 days later and are able to hunt alone when two months old. FAMILY: Mustelidae, ORDER: Carnivora, CLASS: Mammalia. N.D.

STOATS CHARMING. A few people have been fortunate enough to see stoats at play, giving accounts of how these lithe, agile animals twist and turn like snakes, writhe, roll, leapfrog over each other, jump high in the air and even box each other with their forepaws. This behaviour seems to be as fascinating to other animals as to man; J. G. Millais, famous for his voluminous *History of British Mammals,* describes seeing some 50

The stoat, a member of the weasel family, is famous for the use of its white winter coat, with its black-tipped tail, as the ermine of royalty and nobility.

rabbits sitting around and watching a stoat playing in front of them. Suddenly the stoat rushed at one of the rabbits, bowled it over and worried it. Yet the rabbit appeared unhurt and unconcerned. More often, however, the accounts end with the stoat making a sudden dash at one of its audience and killing it. It has been suggested that the stoat is 'charming' its prey, attracting the attention of animals which are first impelled by curiosity to watch and then held spellbound while the stoat gambols nearer and nearer until it is within striking distance. Such behaviour has also been observed in martens and weasels, as well as foxes.

STOCKFISH *Merluccius capensis*, the South African cod and member of the same genus as the North Atlantic cod. The stockfish is the most important element in South African trawl fisheries, far exceeding other fishes in both numbers and weight. In 1959–60 the catch amounted to 150 million lb (68 million kg). In Europe and America the name stockfish is generally used to denote cod that have been split and hung up to dry. FAMILY: Gadidae, ORDER: Gadiformes, CLASS: Pisces.

STOMACH, a wide, and usually distensible, part of the alimentary canal concerned with the temporary storage of food and with digestion. One of its important functions is to even out the flow of material through the gut. In most vertebrates the stomach has well developed muscle layers and its churning movements, together with the action of enzymes and weak hydrochloric acid secreted by the gastric glands of the stomach wall, bring about, or complete, the mechanical and chemical breakdown of large pieces of food into a fine, watery mixture known as chyme. The outlet into the intestine is controlled by a circular muscle, the pyloric sphincter, by means of which the flow of chyme into the intestine is regulated.

STONE CRABS, at a superficial glance very like *Spider crabs yet they are not true crabs. If the abdomen of a female is examined it is found to be asymmetrical, with the appendages missing on the right hand side. This is an indication that Stone crabs have evolved from Hermit crabs, but they have redeveloped hard plates on the abdomen which is held tucked forwards under the thorax. The last pair of legs is reduced in size and hidden between the thorax and abdomen. This characteristic is shared with the Porcelain crabs and the Squat lobsters, and places the Stone crabs firmly in the suborder Anomura.

Stone crabs are mainly cold-water creatures and only enter shallow waters when these are cool throughout the year. There is only one species of the family around the

British coast. This is *Lithodes maia*, which has a geographical range extending from the Canadian coast to Spitzbergen and down the coast of Europe to Belgium. In the North Pacific the *King crab, a relative of Stone crabs, forms the basis of an important fishery. FAMILY: Lithodidae, SUBORDER: Anomura, ORDER: Decapoda, CLASS: Crustacea, PHYLUM: Arthropoda.

STONE-CURLEWS, an almost cosmopolitan family of large wading birds some of which are alternatively called 'thick-knees'. The family includes nine species of medium-sized to rather large birds, 14–20 in (35–51 cm) long, classified in three genera, two of which contain only one species. They are found in Europe, temperate and tropical Africa, Australia and Asia and in tropical America. The northern species migrate to warmer areas for the winter. Birds of open country, they are found on stony or sandy ground, sea-shores, along sandy river-beds and on grassy savannahs. One species, the Southern stone-curlew *Burhinus magnirostris* of Australia, is found in scrub and open woodland. There is evidence that it breeds in cover, but moves into more open areas to feed.

Stone-curlews bear a superficial resemblance to bustards, another group of birds found in open country, but their real relationships are with the waders, plovers and gulls included in the varied assemblage of the order Charadriiformes. They have long un-feathered legs, long wings and large eyes. They hunt at dusk or by night and they remain crouched in concealment during the daylight hours. When disturbed they run swiftly and their flight is strong, though it is usually brief and infrequent. The plumage is of varied shades of concealing grey, brown and buff, with broad stripes on the side of the head.

The bill is short and plover-like in the seven species of the genus *Burhinus;* longer than the head, heavy and swollen in the Beach stone-curlew *Orthorhamphus magnirostris* from Australia and islands nearby, and similarly long and massive in the Great stone-curlew *Esacus magnirostris* of India, but in this species it is slightly upturned at the tip. All of the species that have been studied feed on large insects, small reptiles and amphibians, crustaceans, molluscs, worms, nestling birds and small mammals.

A clutch of one or two rounded, cryptically-marked eggs is laid either directly on the ground or in a small unlined hollow. The eggs are incubated by both parents, though the female usually takes a larger share. In some species she receives little or no help from the male. The young are very active within a few hours of hatching and soon leave the nest-area. Both parents tend them

for a number of weeks. The Water thick-knee *Burhinus vermiculatus* often nests on the breeding grounds of crocodiles on the banks and muddy islands of African rivers. It would appear that nesting among these large, dangerous reptiles protects their eggs and young from other predators.

Shy, inconspicuous birds as they lie concealed by day, stone-curlews become active and noisy at night. Their nocturnal calls consist of eerie, mournful notes with great carrying power; though cackling, piping and croaking calls have also been described. The Double-striped thick-knee *Burhinus bistria-* *tus,* found in Central and South America is often caught when young and kept as a pet. It becomes tame and confiding, and functions as an admirable watch-dog at night. However, some of the African thick-knees suffer badly at the hands of man. They have developed the habit of resting and feeding on metalled roads, which in tropical areas retain some of their heat at night and attract insects. These birds are often killed as they are dazzled into inactivity by motor vehicle headlights and then run over. FAMILY: Burhinidae, ORDER: Charadriiformes, CLASS: Aves. D.H.

The Stone curlew is distinguished by its large yellow eye and prominent leg joint which in England has earned it the nickname 'thick-knee'.

STONEFISH *Synanceja verrucosa*, the most venomous of all the scorpionfishes. It is a bottom-living species of the Indo-Pacific region most often found off the coasts of Australia and South Africa. The heavy and ugly body, up to 14 in (35 cm) long, is covered by warts and small flaps of skin that render it almost invisible against a background of rock or coral or if the fish is partly buried in sand. The poisonous dorsal spines are quite capable of killing a man. FAMILY: Synancejidae, ORDER: Scorpaeniformes, CLASS: Pisces.

STONEFISH POISON. Stonefishes are without doubt one of the nastiest animals one can meet. One medical writer described the effects of the venom: 'excruciating pain dominates the clinical picture in the early stages'; or put more graphically by another author: the patient is 'screaming and half mad with agony' which morphine does not relieve. There are reports of victims lashing out madly at anyone who tries to help and, if death does not intervene, the pain may last up to 12 hours before diminishing and it may be a year before recovery is complete.

STONEFLIES, highly characteristic freshwater insects of a primitive order, the Plecoptera. They form one of the most primitive orders of winged insects living today and bear a very close resemblance to fossil stoneflies which were abundant in the Carboniferous period, which ended 270 million years ago.

Adult stoneflies are stout-bodied insects about 1 in (2·5 cm) long, brownish or yellowish, with fore- and hindwings alike in size and shape. They are characterized by having long filamentous antennae and a pair of prominent cerci projecting from the hind end of the abdomen. Stoneflies are well distributed in the northern and southern hemispheres where they are found in cooler hilly areas. Their larvae, with only a few exceptions, live in flowing water, usually in clear, unpolluted stony streams where their high consumption of oxygen is readily satisfied by the fast flowing water. The adults can be found in Britain from May to July on vegetation close to streams and rivers. They do not fly well and only emerge on bright days. The eggs are laid directly into water by the females as they crawl on the stream bank or over stones in the stream. Stonefly larvae can be distinguished from mayfly larvae because they have three-segmented tarsi, each with two claws and only two cerci at the end of the abdomen. Mayfly larvae have three caudal cerci and a one-segmented tarsus, each with a single claw. Furthermore, the gills of stoneflies are either on the thorax or between the legs while those of mayflies are

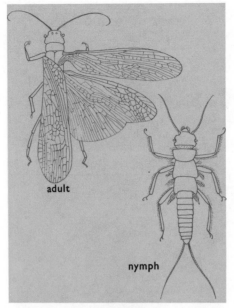

Adult and nymph of a stonefly *Perla* differ little except for the wings in the adult.

arranged along the sides of the abdomen. The larvae are generally found beneath stones or in dense water-weeds. They are not ready swimmers. The smaller species like *Nemoura* feed on green algae and the remains of plants while the larger ones, such as *Perla* are voracious carnivores and feed on worms, rotifers, small crustaceans and other insect larvae. Stonefly larvae are very similar to the adults in appearance, especially as they mature and their wing buds enlarge. They leave the water to metamorphose directly into adults without a pupal stage. Most British species take a year to develop from egg to adult but the larger *Perla* and *Dinocras* take as long as three years. Several stonefly species have been imitated by fishermen with their artificial flies and are thus known by popular names; for example, *Isoperla grammatica* is known as the Yellow Sally, *Taeniopteryx nebulosa* as the February Red and *Protonemura meyeri* as the Early Brown. The nymphs of Perlidae and Perlodidae are known as creepers. ORDER: Plecoptera, CLASS: Insecta, PHYLUM: Arthropoda. R.C.F.

STORKS, large, sometimes very large, birds of heavy build, with long legs, long necks, wings that are both long and broad and long, stout, pointed bills which may be either straight or turned up or down. The plumage is commonly black and white, in a bold pattern, and some species have bright red bill and legs. They are related to the herons (Ardeidae), ibises (Threskiornithidae) and other groups, in some of which the name 'stork' is also applied. The storks themselves constitute the family Ciconiidae, which is divided into two subfamilies: the typical storks (Ciconiinae) and the so-called Wood ibises (Mycteriinae), with 13 species in the former and four in the latter.

The family is widely represented in the tropics and subtropics of the Old World and two species breed in the temperate zone of Europe and Asia, performing long migrations from there. A single species is found, not exclusively, in Australia but there is none in New Zealand. Only three species belong to the New World, and none of them to its higher latitudes.

Storks are adapted, in general, to wading in shallow water or walking in marshes; the long legs and slightly webbed feet being adaptations for this. They mostly find their food in such situations, but some species feed on drier ground. The food consists largely of freshwater animals and of large insects, but three species feed mainly on carrion. Storks fly strongly, with extended neck and trailing legs in most species. Some are notably adept at soaring in thermal air-currents. They tend to be gregarious at all seasons and large flocks may be seen. Various display attitudes can be observed. In a characteristic greeting ceremony between mates at the nest, both birds bend the neck backwards until the head touches the top of the body. Most species are vocally silent, or nearly so, but a noisy clattering of the mandibles is common.

Storks most commonly nest in trees, but sometimes on cliffs or buildings, breeding in colonies if the availability of sites permits. The nest is usually a bulky platform of sticks. The eggs are white, or almost so, and there are usually three to six in a clutch. The young are hatched almost naked, but a plumage of down is soon grown and it is a feature of the group that this is succeeded by a second down plumage before this, in its turn, gives way to true feathers. The young take a few years to reach breeding maturity. Both sexes share in incubating and rearing the young.

The White stork *Ciconia ciconia,* of which there are several geographical subspecies, is the most familiar member of the group and also the one that has been most closely studied scientifically. It nests chiefly on buildings and it finds much of its food on cultivated land. Being generally esteemed as beneficial to man, it shows little fear; and it is so conspicuous that it is easily observed. It thus makes an almost ideal subject for population studies. Unhappily these confirm the impression that its numbers are greatly diminishing in most European countries. It is still found as far north as the Netherlands and Denmark, and eastwards through Germany and Russia to Asia. It was never a regular inhabitant of the British Isles and it has ceased to be one in Sweden. Southwards, it breeds in Spain and Portugal, North Africa and also in southeastern Europe and again eastwards, but not in Italy.

The White stork is a notable migrant, and in many places the movements can be

The Painted stork of India.

readily seen in progress—large birds flying by day in flocks, and often making use of the upward air-currents over the warm land. The species has also been ringed, mostly nestlings, on a large scale. The European population winters in Africa south of the Sahara, many of the birds going as far as Cape Province. Of the latter, a few sporadically remain to breed and immature birds may also linger in winter-quarters. The more easterly populations migrate to southern Asia.

The migrants from northern and Central Europe usually fly southeastwards to Asia Minor and then follow the coast of the Levant to Egypt, sea-crossings being very largely avoided. Birds from farther east in Europe seem to reach Africa by way of Iraq and Arabia. The route, farther south through East Africa to the eastern part of South Africa, is well marked both by observations and by ringing records. Great numbers may interrupt their journey in East Africa when plagues of locusts offer abundant food. On the other hand, birds native to the extreme

western part of the European range (roughly, west of the River Weser) tend to migrate southwestwards to the Iberian Peninsula and, together with the birds breeding in Spain and Portugal, reach Africa from there. The birds breeding in North Africa also cross the Sahara.

The Black stork *C. nigra* has a breeding distribution roughly similar to that of its more familiar relative, and it performs equivalent migrations. In some respects, however, it provides a decided contrast. In appearance it differs in the dark plumage of its upperparts, being very dark brown, glossed with a metallic sheen of copper, green and purple. In habits it differs in being an inhabitant of deep forest, where it nests in tall trees beside clearings where pools or marshes provide opportunity for feeding. The nest is particularly large and usually placed in a pine, at the level of the first large branches rather than at the top. A few thick sticks are placed as a foundation for a platform of thinner ones which the birds weave in and out with their bills. This forms

a bowl, which is then filled with moss and soft herbage. Both birds take part in this work. An old nest that has survived the winter may be repaired in preference to building a new one. Sometimes the abandoned nest of a bird of prey will be appropriated.

The Black stork is much less numerous than the White and is likewise decreasing. The European range is also more restricted and on migration relatively fewer birds seem to penetrate beyond the Equator. A small resident population, however, has become established in South Africa, where the birds breed on mountain cliffs in the southern winter.

Abdim's stork *Sphenorynchus abdimii* is a migrant of a different sort, performing extensive movements almost entirely within Africa south of the Sahara. It breeds in the early part of the rainy season (from April onwards) in the northern tropical belt from Senegal to Somalia and also in East Africa as far south as northern Tanzania. In the non-breeding season some birds visit Arabia, but most perform a trans-equatorial migration and the species becomes widespread in the southern parts of the continent, being thus a non-breeding summer visitor to South Africa (from October). It is a common species, sometimes seen in flocks of several hundred birds.

Abdim's stork is one of the smaller members of the family, standing little more than 2 ft (0·6 m) high. Its plumage is mainly dark, but the white belly is a conspicuous character. The bill is green. It is a tame bird, often found about villages and building its nest of sticks on huts as well as in trees. It feeds to a large extent on locusts, but also on rodents, reptiles, frogs and fishes. It has a feeble piping call.

The saddlebill (sometimes misnamed 'jabiru') *Ephippiorhynchus senegalensis* is another African species, widely distributed in the tropics but not numerous. It is a large long-legged bird, standing more than 4 ft (1·2 m) high. It takes its name from a black band round the middle of its heavy red bill. The plumage is black and white, the sexes being alike except for the curious fact that the male has a brown iris, toning with the feathers of the head, whereas the female has a conspicuous chrome-yellow iris. The bird feeds in shallow water after the manner of the heron. The attitude in flight is, so to speak, bent, the extended neck and trailing legs both incline downwards at an angle from the body.

Two species of openbill (or Open-billed stork) *Anastomus lamelligerus* and *A. oscitans* are found, respectively, in tropical Africa and Madagascar and in southern

The White stork winters in Africa, and nests on buildings in Europe in summer.

Asia. They are among the smaller storks and have mainly dark plumage. Remarkably the mandibles do not meet along their whole length when the bill is closed. The tips meet, but behind that there is a wide gap extending about half way to the base. This is believed to be an adaptation to extracting and holding large and slippery Water snails. Feeding is largely nocturnal. The nests are placed in reedbeds or low trees.

Anastomus oscitans is the most common stork in India, and Salim Ali has recently (1968) given this vivid description of their return from a period of soaring on the thermal air-currents in company with other species: 'The descent from aloft is a spectacular performance. With erect neck, head held high (cocked), wings half pulled in, the dangling legs partly flexed and straddled to balance—sometimes worked back and forth as in running—the bird hurtles steeply through space, banking, side-slipping and gyrating violently, till within a few short seconds, from a mere speck in the sky, it has swished down to alight buoyantly on a tree-top in the colony, preceded by a vigorous braking with the wings'.

The Woolly-necked stork (or Bishop stork) *Dissoura episcopus* is distributed both in Africa and in southern Asia, as far east as Borneo. The upper plumage is mainly iridescent black, but the feathers of the neck are white and have a 'woolly' appearance. In other respects this species is rather similar to Abdim's stork. It is not a very common bird and its habits are not well known. It differs from most of its family in having a harsh raucous cry.

The Black-necked stork *Xenorhynchus asiaticus* is not an African species, but is found from India to Australia, being in the latter the sole representative of the family. It is a large species, with mainly dark plumage and a slightly upturned bill. Hume, long ago (1890), described the greeting display ceremony of the Black-necked stork: 'A pair will gravely stalk up to each other and when about a yard or 2 ft (90–60 cm) apart will stand face to face, extend their long black and white wings, and while they flutter these very rapidly, so that the points of the wings of the one flap against the points of the other's wings, advance their heads until they nearly meet, and both simultaneously clatter their bills like a couple of watchmen's rattles'. This description cannot be bettered today.

The marabou *Leptoptilos crumeniferus* of Africa, together with the adjutant *L. dubius* and Lesser adjutant *L. javanicus* of southern

Yellow-billed stork of Kenya probably has the most sensitive bill of all birds. It can catch its food – fishes and other small swimming animals – by feeling them swimming by.

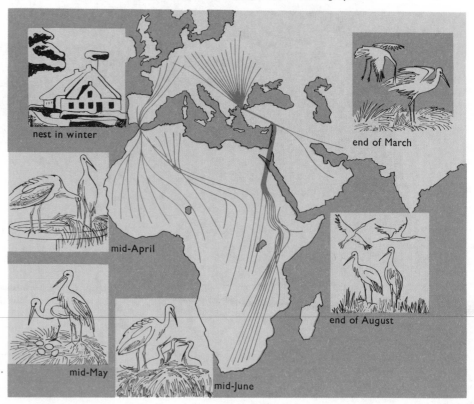

Migration routes of the stork, with (inset) stages in their breeding, from the end of March when they fly north to their nests to the end of August when parents and young fly south.

Asia, have been dealt with separately. These are very large storks and eat carrion.

Turning to the New World, we find the jabiru *Jabiru mycteria* distributed from southern Mexico to Argentina. This is a large species and the heavy bill is slightly upturned at the tip. The plumage is mainly white, but the head and upper neck are featherless and the exposed skin is blue-black with some orange and red on the lower part of the area. The jabiru is less gregarious than most storks, but flocks are formed on occasion. It nests in tall palm trees. Although in general appearance it somewhat resembles the adjutant, it is not a scavenger but hunts for small animals in shallow water.

The Maguari stork *Euxenura galeata* is common in Argentina and other parts of South America. It is of medium size, for a stork, and has mainly white plumage but with black on the wings and above the tail. It lives on small animals, found either in shallow water or on the dry ground of the pampae and fields.

The Wood ibis of the subfamily Mycteriinae, a name now applied to only one of the four species in the subfamily is really a misnomer since there is no close relationship with the true ibises of the family Threskiornithidae, the main point of resemblance being the decurved (but less markedly decurved) bill. In general appearance the four species are obviously storks.

The Wood ibis *Ibis ibis* of tropical Africa resembles the White stork in size and to some extent in plumage, but the tail is black, and instead of being red the bill is orange and the legs are pink. A conspicuous feature, in addition to the shape of the bill, is the bare red face. The species is widely distributed and the trees containing its nesting colonies are often found in villages or even towns. It appears to live mainly on fishes.

The Painted stork *I. leucocephalus* of India and other parts of southern Asia is a similar species, but the bare skin of the face is orange-yellow; there is also a dark band across the chest. The nesting colonies sometimes contain several thousands of pairs, usually mixed with other species of like habits. The birds tend to disperse in quest of food, unless the source is particularly abundant. The Southern painted stork *I. cinereus* is found from Malaya to Java.

The Wood stork (or Wood ibis) *Mycteria americana* is found from the southern United States and the Greater Antilles southwards to Argentina. It is a large bird with mainly white plumage, but with black on wings and tail, and the bare skin of the head and upper neck is black. It breeds in trees, notably cypresses, in swampy areas and a colony may contain a few thousand pairs and every tree be crowded with nests. The general habits resemble those of the Old World species. It has been described as

sometimes feeding in echelon in shallow water, in a co-operative way so that each bird disturbs prey that may be caught by the next if not by itself. FAMILY: Ciconiidae, ORDER: Ciconiiformes, CLASS: Aves. A.L.T.

STORK VIRTUES. The story of storks bringing babies is not to be found in the writings of the old authors of the 16th century or earlier, so it is a more recent fable; it appears in Hans Anderson's writings. The stork has, however, been associated with man for a long time as it nests on buildings and the Ancient Egyptians respected it as a scavenger. To have a stork nest on the roof was considered lucky and the Dutch once believed that if a stork was encouraged to nest on a house it would leave one of the young ones for the owner. The return of a stork to the same nest and mate each year made the stork a symbol of fidelity and it was thought that when one became old it was cared for by its offspring.

STORM PETRELS, the smallest of all seabirds forming a distinct group within the Procellariiformes, separated from the albatrosses, shearwaters and true petrels by having the prominent tube-nostrils fused into a single external opening. The group is divided into two subfamilies, the Hydrobatinae and Oceanitinae. The former are mainly northerly breeding species which have long pointed wings, usually forked tails and short legs whereas the latter are southern hemisphere forms with shorter and more rounded wings, square tails, slimmer bills and characteristically very elongated legs. All are small being 5–10 in (12–25 cm) long. The long-legged species are adapted for pattering along on the surface of the water while picking up small fishes and planktonic crustaceans. This, and the belief among sailors that they herald rough weather, is responsible for their common name. The other mariners' name of Mother Cary's chickens is thought to come from Mater Cara after the Blessed Virgin Mary. These two subfamilies may have evolved in isolation, the northerly forms perhaps deriving from a migratory southern species, but now there is considerable overlap in the tropics. Many of the species breeding in high latitudes have considerable migrations. Wilson's storm petrel *Oceanites oceanicus* breeds all round Antarctica and winters in the tropics and as far north as Britain and Newfoundland.

All Storm petrels are social birds and breed in colonies, usually on islands, where there are no mammalian predators. Hornby's storm petrel *Oceanodroma hornbyi*, however, breeds inland in the coastal mountains of Chile. With the single

exception of *O. tethys,* all species are nocturnal in their visits to land, perhaps mainly to avoid predatory birds but also allowing them to feed during the day. The single white egg is so large, up to $\frac{1}{4}$ of the bird's weight, that it must be a considerable strain for the female to produce and lay even this one egg. Studies on several species have indicated that the adults are incapable of feeding more than a single young and, even if they could, it is doubtful if the female could produce two eggs of this size. The sexes incubate in turn and the egg hatches after about 42 days. On hatching, the young is covered in long down which is usually replaced by a second coat as the young grows. Development is slow, but at its peak the young weighs half as much again as the adult. The chick fledges after about 8–10 weeks. The accumulation of fat by the young allows it to survive if food becomes short. This, and the slow growth, are probably necessary if the adults are to raise even a single chick on a poor, or erratic, food supply.

The Madeiran storm petrel *O. castro* is unique among seabirds as in one area there are two separate populations which share the same nest-hole but breed six months out of phase. Each bird has an annual breeding cycle and there is no interchange of breeders or non-breeders between the two populations. If this separation is associated with young birds returning to breed at the time of year when they were raised, two different forms could quickly arise. FAMILY: Hydrobatidae, ORDER: Procellariifromes, CLASS: Aves.   M.P.H.

STURGEONS, primitive, often large fishes from temperate waters of the northern hemisphere, descended from the ancient palaeoniscids (see fishes, fossil). The dense bony skeleton of the palaeoniscids has, however, been replaced by cartilage, the scales have been lost and the dermal armour is represented by a series of bony plates or bucklers. The biting mouth is now an underslung, protrusile sucking mouth. The sturgeons are, however, larger than their ancestors, some reaching well over 20 ft (6 m) in length. Although not related, the sturgeons have a rather shark-like appearance which is heightened by the steeply rising tail.

Sturgeons are found throughout most of the cold and temperate waters of the northern hemisphere, some species living in the sea and migrating up rivers to spawn, while others live permanently in rivers or are landlocked in lakes. There are about 25 species, all rather slow-moving that browse on the bottom. Fleshy barbels surround the mouth and are used to detect prey (usually bottom-living invertebrates). There is a spiral valve in the intestine, a primitive feature also found in the sharks.

The largest of the sturgeons is the beluga

Huso huso of the Volga and the Black and Caspian Seas for which a length of 28 ft (8·4 m) and a weight of 2,860 lb (1,300 kg) have been recorded. A related species, *H. dauricus* from the Amur basin and the Far East, is smaller. The Atlantic sturgeons all belong to the genus *Acipenser*. The largest from the New World is the White sturgeon *A. transmontanus* of the Pacific coasts of North America which now grows to about 300 lb (135 kg) but in the past has been known to reach over 1,200 lb (540 kg). These fishes rarely go to sea until they are almost mature, the younger individuals living in rivers and migrating up and down stream each winter and spring.

The common Atlantic sturgeon *A. sturio* reaches a weight of 700 lb (315 kg), although the males are smaller. They live in the sea and migrate into rivers to spawn. Formerly widespread and occurring in most European rivers, Atlantic populations now survive only in the Guadalquivir in Spain, the rivers of the Gironde in France and Lake Ladoga in the Soviet Union. Stragglers may reach Great Britain but by ancient right they are royal fish and belong to the monarch. Some of the American sturgeons are confined to lakes, for example the Shovel-nose sturgeon *Scaphirhynchus platyrhynchus,* a species with a long and flattened snout.

Sturgeon are valuable commercial fishes, particularly prized for the eggs or caviar removed from fishes migrating up rivers to spawn. The eggs are separated and soaked in salt, the quality of the caviar being determined by the length of time the eggs are soaked and the strength of the brine. The swimbladders are an important source of isinglass, the skin is tanned and the bony plates are used for ornaments. The flesh is delicious and although caviar is extremely expensive it is possible to buy sturgeon cuts quite cheaply.

Beluga that are not caught as they migrate up rivers continue upstream to spawn in deep holes. Such migratory sturgeon have definite breeding seasons but the Lake sturgeon *A. fulvescens* of the United States has continuously ripening eggs. The age of large sturgeon is of great interest to the fisheries and it is recorded that a Russian fish weighing almost a ton (1,000 kg) was estimated to be 75 years old. FAMILY: Acipenseridae, ORDER: Acipenseriformes, CLASS: Pisces.

SUBSONG, a quiet song produced by many songbirds, particularly at the beginning of the breeding season before the full song has developed. It tends to have notes of lower frequency than normal song but is produced in longer sequences. Subsong tends to have a different general structure from the full song but nevertheless seems to contain the raw materials from which the full song is later developed.

SUCKERS or Shark suckers, a family of fishes with a dorsal fin modified into a powerful sucker for attachment to other fishes, turtles or boats. They are more usually known as *remoras.

SUGARBIRDS, a genus of two species of small, long-tailed perching birds peculiar to southern Africa and not extending farther north than Rhodesia. They are thought by some ornithologists to be an isolated part of the mainly Australian family of honey-eaters (Meliphagidae). Sugarbirds are rather plainly coloured with a yellow vent, long, curved, rather slender bills and long tail feathers. The tail feathers of the male are considerably longer than those of the female, being about 12 in (30 cm) of the total length of the bird, which is 17 in (43 cm).

Both species, the Cape sugarbird *Promerops cafer* and Gurney's sugarbird *P. gurnei* are limited to those areas where *Protea* form a dominant element in the vegetation. The Cape sugarbird is confined to the southern and eastern mountainous regions of the Cape, while the Gurney's sugarbird is found in mountainous regions of the eastern Cape, Natal, eastern and north-eastern Transvaal, recurring in eastern Rhodesia. Both species feed on insects, spiders and honey and most of this food is obtained from the flower heads of the *Protea*. However, many an insect or spider is also extracted from between the rather densely packed *Protea* leaves, by the thorough food-searching activities of these birds. Although at certain times, especially when the *Protea* does not flower, sugarbirds may temporarily vacate the *Protea*-clad mountain slopes, there is no doubt that their feeding behaviour is closely associated with *Protea*.

The Cape sugarbird's breeding season falls mainly in the southern winter (March to August, with a peak in May). This coincides with the main flowering season for most of the *Protea*. During the breeding season the Cape sugarbird is strongly territorial. Any intruder is immediately chased out by the male. This is usually done by threat behaviour, that is the male perches near the intruder singing loudly and this is usually sufficient to chase the other bird away. Actual fighting is very rare. The nest is a cup, rather untidy on the outside but neat on the inside. In about 57% of cases the nest is built in a *Protea* bush itself and when this does not happen there are always *Protea* bushes in the close vicinity. It is the female which builds the nest and there are indications that she also chooses the actual nest-site. The building material is very constant, the bulk of the nest consisting of twigs, mainly heather, sometimes mixed with dry grass or bracken. The lining is always formed of a thick layer of brown *Protea*-seed fluff. In seven observed cases it took the female from five to ten days to build the nest. The eggs are cryptically coloured greyish brown with a number of darker streaks and blotches. The normal clutch is two eggs and the first is laid in the early morning hours

The common Atlantic sturgeon lives in the sea but enters rivers to spawn.

and the second around mid-day. Incubation starts after the second egg has been laid. Only the female incubates. The male may visit the nest but will never sit on the eggs, spending all its time feeding in the top of *Protea* bushes, defending the territory against intruders and advertizing the fact that the territory is occupied. It also indulges in a rather characteristic flight, moving unevenly through the air with the long tail jerking and spreading behind. While in flight it utters a special call.

The eggs hatch on the 17th day of incubation usually in the afternoon. After both eggs have hatched the female continues to brood for a considerable time but there is a gradual decrease until the sixth day when the chicks are left uncovered during the day. However, the female still covers them at night for a further two weeks. By this time the feathers of the chicks are fairly well developed. Both parents feed the chicks but observations have shown that on an average 76% of the feeding is done by the female. As is common in most birds the faeces of the young are removed by the parents. It seems that they fly with the faeces to the fringe of their territory and usually deposit them on particular *Protea* bushes. The chicks are fed on insects, spiders and, especially when they are very young, on nectar. The sugarbird's tongue is very long, rolled up at the sides and can be protruded to suck up nectar. When the parent bird catches a fairly large insect it kills it by taking it in its bill and repeatedly hitting it against a branch. Sugarbirds sometimes catch their prey on the wing by darting in flycatcher fashion from a perch. The nestling period lasts from 17 to 21 days. On average, therefore, five weeks elapse from the onset of incubation to departure of the young from the nest.

It is difficult to obtain information on how long the young sugarbirds are fed by the parents after leaving the nest, as this species lives in rather bushy terrain and it is not easy to keep young under observation. However, it is probable that the post-nestling stage is about 21 days.

Sugarbirds sometimes have two broods in one season and in a few cases it was observed that the female was sitting on a second clutch while the male was still feeding the chicks of the first clutch. There is considerable variation in the actual spot chosen by the same female to build her nest even in the same season, but colour ringing showed that the same territory is used in subsequent years. The mortality of eggs and young in a species like the Cape sugarbird, which breeds during the cold rainy season, can be rather high because, in addition to predators, they suffer from the adverse climatic conditions. It was found that the total mortality of eggs and young in this species was as high as 67%.

The male Cape sugarbird, with his very long tail, perched on a Protea flowerhead.

Female Cape sugarbird feeding chicks.

Cape sugarbirds will occasionally have a bath in the tops of *Protea* bushes when the latter are wet after rain. When doing so the bird flaps its wings and, keeping them above its back, it rubs its head and neck against the wet leaves and also spreads its tail. These movements are quick and will dislodge water drops from the leaves which then shower onto the bird.

The habits of Gurney's sugarbird are similar to those of the Cape sugarbird, but there are some differences. For instance where the Cape sugarbird, on the whole, allows the observer to come very near, Gurney's sugarbird is very timid and unlike the Cape sugarbird, Gurney's breeds in the early summer from October to November. FAMILY: Promeropidae, ORDER: Passeriformes, CLASS: Aves.   G.J.B.

SUNBEAM SNAKE *Xenopeltis unicolor*, placed in a family of its own, is a harmless snake with many primitive features suggesting affinities with *Pipe snakes and *boas but in other respects it shows resemblances to the more highly evolved snakes. The broad blunt head with small eye and large symmetrical head shield merges into the trunk without a neck constriction. The belly scales are broad. There are no vestiges of a pelvis, but two lungs are developed, the left half the size of the right. The skull is solid with the snout firmly joined to the cranium. The upper jaw bones are more firmly attached to each other than in more highly evolved snakes and the gape is limited. The popular name of this largely brown snake stems from its shiny iridescent scales. *Xenopeltis* grows to 4 ft (122 cm), is widely distributed, but not common, from Burma to southern China and the Malay Archipelago, on mountains and in lowlands and even cultivated districts. It feeds on lizards, frogs, rodents, and other snakes. If molested it vibrates its tail rapidly. FAMILY: Xenopeltidae, ORDER: Squamata, CLASS: Reptilia.

SUNBIRDS, tiny brilliantly coloured birds belonging to the family Nectariniidae which also includes the spiderhunters.

They are the Old World equivalent of the American hummingbirds, although they cannot match the latter in beauty, powers of flight, or minuteness, and are not related to them. The smallest of the hundred or so species of sunbirds is $3\frac{3}{4}$ in (10 cm) long, the largest over 8 in (21 cm). All have lightly-built bodies, slim, delicate legs and strong feet. The bill is fine and long and in many species it is strongly curved downwards. The tongue is tubular along part of its length as an adaptation to nectar-feeding. Most male sunbirds are brilliantly coloured with green, purple or bronze metallic colours on

Male Palestine sunbird *Nectarinia osea*.

the breast and upperparts and a non-metallic, though often colourful, belly. In a few species, such as the widespread Beautiful sunbird *Nectarinia pulchella* of Africa, the central tail feathers are greatly elongated. Female sunbirds are usually dull brown or olive. In some species, the males moult into a dull plumage outside the breeding season and then resemble the females. Many male sunbirds, and some females too, have small patches of bright red, orange, or yellow feathers (called pectoral tufts) on the sides of the breast. Though normally hidden, these tufts can be erected during display.

The greatest variety of sunbirds (66 species) is found in Africa (Kenya alone boasts 15). There are four species in Arabia, and one reaches Palestine. Sunbirds are widely distributed in the warmer parts of Asia and a small number have reached New Guinea and northern Australia.

Sunbirds are found in many kinds of vegetation: lowland and montane tropical forests, mangrove swamps, savannah and even semi-desert, wherever there are trees or shrubs providing sufficient nectar and insect food. A surprising number of sunbirds are in fact montane dwellers. Several live between 4,000–9,000 ft (1,200–2,750 m) in Africa and the Himalayas and one, the Scarlet-tufted malachite sunbird *Nectarinia johnstoni*, has been seen above 12,000 ft (3,650 m) in the Ruwenzori Mts. Some species are very tame and live, sometimes in large numbers, in the heart of towns and cities where they feed on ornamental trees and garden flowers. The males, especially, are very noisy, pugnacious birds, chasing one another a great deal.

The nests of sunbirds are delicate, oval structures with a small entrance hole near the top on one side and often there is a small 'porch' over the entrance. The nesting material varies, but is usually fibres, rootlets, dead leaf fragments etc, bound together with cobwebs. The lining is of softer material such as kapok, or other vegetable down, and may be very thick. Nests are attached to the tips of branches, or roots projecting from a bank. Where they live in close association with man, the trailing end of a piece of barbed wire or aerial may be used as a nest site. The usual clutch is two eggs, occasionally three.

Sunbirds are mostly arboreal, though some will feed on flowers near ground-level. They are extremely active and spend most of their time visiting flowers, which they probe for nectar, and searching for the small spiders and insects which provide their main food. When visiting garden flowers too deep for the nectar to be reached in the usual way, a sunbird may pierce the corolla near the base and reach the nectar in that way. The hole made is minute and does little real damage to the flower.

Sunbird *Nectarinia*, one of 66 species most of which are concentrated in Africa.

Some species, especially those living in drier regions, perform local migrations to take advantage of peak flowering periods in different areas. FAMILY: Nectariniidae, ORDER: Passeriformes, CLASS: Aves.   P.W.

SUNBITTERN *Eurypyga helias,* South American wading bird resembling a small heron. Sunbittern is the common name for the family Eurypygidae in which there is only the single species. It has a wide distribution, occurring from Mexico south throughout Central and South America to eastern Peru, southeastern Brazil and Bolivia.

Sunbitterns are about 18 in (45 cm) long, have long thin necks, dagger-like bills, long legs, broad tails and broad wings. The plumage is full and soft, almost like that of an owl, and is barred and mottled grey and brown. The crown is black with a distinct white streak above and below the eyes. When the bird spreads its wings a pattern of black, chestnut and yellow becomes visible. On the tail there are two bands of black and chestnut. The eyes are red. The upper mandible is black and the lower one yellow. The feet are orange-yellow.

Sunbitterns live along overgrown creeks and rivers in the tropical rain-forest and are often to be seen wading with slow movements through the shallow water of a creek, stopping suddenly, looking intensely into the water and with a quick dart of the bill seizing prey. Their food consists to a large

extent of water insects and their larvae, creatures such as Water beetles, flies and the larvae of dragonflies, but they also eat small snails, crabs and fishes.

They spend a large amount of time on the ground, but perch in trees when disturbed. They can swim and will cross creeks in this way.

They are a beautiful sight when they spread their wings wide and fan out their tails. This is usually considered to be part of their courting display but it is also a kind of threatening pose. A young bird kept by the author for some time would spread its wings in this way each time an attempt was made to handle it.

On the whole sunbitterns are silent birds but will sometimes utter a soft whistle and a rattling note when alarmed. The flight is noiseless like that of an owl. They are often seen in zoos and these specimens are probably taken as young birds from the nest by Indians and sold to zoo collectors.

Though not uncommon in its range very little is known about the sunbittern's life in the wild. This is partly due to the lack of observers but also to the bird's secluded life along streams in dark forest where it is difficult to see. Not many nests have been found, but the American ornithologist, Alexander Skutch, has described a nest he saw in March 1969, in Costa Rica. It was a large, bulky, globular structure about 20 ft (6 m) up on a sloping side branch of a slender tree near a forest stream. It was made of decaying leaves and stems with a small amount of green moss and apparently some mud. The bird was sitting on two eggs. The eggs were pinkish buff with a number of brown spots and measured about $1\frac{3}{4} \times 1\frac{1}{2}$ in (4.4×3.4 cm).

As long ago as 1865 a pair nested in the London Zoo and then three eggs were laid which were incubated by both parents for 27 days and the downy nestlings stayed in the nest where both parents fed them. FAMILY: Eurypygidae, ORDER: Gruiformes, CLASS: Aves.   F.H.

SUNFISHES or centrarchids, a family of common freshwater fishes from North America containing the crappies, bluegills and Black basses. The two dozen species are perch-like, with a spinous anterior portion to the dorsal fin and in some species the body is deep and compressed. These fishes are nest builders, the male scooping out a hollow and guarding the eggs once the female has deposited them. The *Black basses (species of *Micropterus*) have been dealt with elsewhere. The crappies (species of *Pomoxis*) from the northeast of the United States, which can grow to 21 inches (54 cm), are popular sport fishes that have now been introduced into fishing waters elsewhere in the country. The White crappie *P. annularis* prefers rather still and turbid waters, whereas the Black crappie *P. nigromaculatus* is generally found in clear waters. The Bluegill sunfishes or bluegills are fairly deep-bodied and are characterized by a bony projection from the upper corner of the gill cover, popularly referred to as an 'ear flap'. The Pumpkinseed bluegill *Lepomis gibbosus* is one of the most colourful and best known species. The back is dark green to olive, the undersides yellow to orange, and there are red, blue and orange spots arranged irregularly on the flanks. There is a brilliant scarlet spot on the 'ear flap', from which this species

derives its common name. It reaches 9 in (23 cm) and is found in the maritime provinces of the United States and Canada. The Green sunfish *L. cyanellus* grows to the same size but is less colourful. The bluegill *L. macrochirus* has been introduced into all the States (except Alaska). Reaching 4 lb (1.8 kg) in weight, the bluegill can be recognized by the bluish colour of the lower jaw, lower part of the cheek and gill cover. The Red-ear sunfish *L. microlophus*, a smaller species, is dull olive with a red band on the gill cover. It is also known as the shell-cracker since it has strong teeth in the throat (pharyngeal teeth) with which it crushes snails on which it feeds. The Spotted sunfish *L. punctatus* is reputed to linger beside tree stumps and half-submerged logs waiting for insects or frogs to settle above it, thereafter charging the log to knock its prey into the water. This has never been verified, however.

The Sacramento perch *Archoplytes interruptus* is the only species of sunfish found naturally in the rivers and streams of the western part of the United States.

The sunfishes, and especially the Black basses and the bluegills, have been introduced into a number of countries outside the United States including the cooler parts of East Africa. FAMILY: Centrarchidae, ORDER: Perciformes, CLASS: Pisces.

SUNGAZER *Cordylus giganteus*, the largest species of the Girdle-tailed lizards, so named for its persistent habit of basking. See cordylid lizards.

SUNI *Neotragus moschatus*, a small brown-grey gazelle, ranging from Natal to Kenya, where it is very localized. See Dwarf antelopes.

SUNSET SHELLS, common intertidal bivalve shells *Tellina tenuis*, so called because of their delicate pink and red colouration. See tellin shells.

The Pumpkinseed bluegill, one of the most colourful of North American sunfishes.

SUNSPIDERS, also called windscorpions or jerrymanders, are terrestrial arachnids of hot dry desert regions. The common name 'sunspider' relates to certain South American species which are active during the daytime, whereas most species are nocturnal. They are relatively large arachnids, up to nearly 3 in (7 cm) in length, superficially similar in appearance to large hairy spiders, but distinguishable from them by the segmented abdomen, or opisthosoma, the absence of spinnerets and the truly massive pair of jaws at the front end of the body. They are very hairy and move across the ground with lightning speed, and this habit, coupled with their ability to bend the abdomen upwards in the manner of a scorpion, has also given them the common

A sunspider *Galeodes citrinus*.

name of 'windscorpion'. During the day, and in winter when they hibernate, sunspiders hide in burrows which they dig in the desert soil by means of their legs and mouthparts. They also possess a remarkable ability, for so large an arachnid, to climb vertical surfaces, and this they do with the aid of sucker-like pads at the tips of the pedipalps, a pair of leg-like appendages attached to the body on either side of the jaws. In addition to the jaws and the pedipalps, the anterior part of the body (cephalothorax or prosoma) also bears four pairs of legs, of which the first pair are long and slender, and are usually extended forwards as feelers, while the remaining three pairs are used for walking and digging. The last pair of legs carry a unique type of

sensory hair, shaped like a miniature tennis racquet, and called a 'racquet organ'.

Sunspiders are voracious carnivores, feeding on insects, woodlice, spiders, scorpions, lizards and even small mice and birds. The pincer-like jaws, which may be as large as the entire prosoma, are used to seize the prey which is macerated into a soft pulp and sucked into the mouth. Feeding will often continue until the gut is so full that the animal can hardly move. Travellers in the desert often come across these arachnids, for they invade tents and sleeping bags, and an encounter with the large hairy body surmounted by massive widely-opened jaws can be a daunting experience. There are many records of these animals biting people, and

the effect is painful although probably not poisonous, despite popular belief.

The 800 or so species of sunspiders can be grouped into 10 families distributed in the tropical and subtropical Americas, Africa, the Middle East and Asia. Half-a-dozen species occur in the Mediterranean region of southern Europe, but the group is absent from Madagascar, Australia and New Zealand. ORDER: Solifugae, CLASS: Arachnida, PHYLUM: Arthropoda. J.A.W.

SUNSTAR, a starfish aptly named, its shape resembling a conventionally drawn sun, with a large disc-like body surrounded by 8–15, most usually 10–12, radiating arms or rays. In America the name is more usually applied

to starfishes of the multi-armed genus *Heliaster*. The colour too is fitting: usually the central disc is purplish-red, the arms whitish with a broad transverse red band, when viewed on the upper or dorsal side; more rarely this side may be purplish all over; the lower or oral side is whitish. The total diameter may reach 14 in (35 cm) but is usually less, the arms being about as long as the disc is broad. The skeleton of the upper surface consists of an irregular network, of narrow calcite bars enclosing fairly large patches of tissue in which little blisters of the body wall known as papulae are found. The skeleton itself bears large broom-shaped groups of rather long, slender spines, the groups sparsely distributed over the upper surface but conspicuously large at the margin.

The Common sunstar *Solaster papposus* is widely distributed over most of the North Atlantic, its southern limit being the English Channel and, on the American coast, approximately latitude 40°N. This or a very similar species is also found in the North Pacific, down the American coast as far south as Vancouver and in the Asian Pacific to the Ochotsch Sea, from low tide mark down to 5,000 ft (1,500 m). *S. endeca*, a rather larger yellowish-red or purple sunstar with more abundant but less conspicuous spine groups on its upper surface, occurs with the same broad geographical distribution, but is known to range down to only some 1,400 ft (450 m). The related *S. dawsoni* and *S. stimpsoni* occur along the northern Pacific coast of North America.

The Common sunstar breeds in March-April in British waters, the female shedding large numbers of eggs into the seawater once the male has spawned. The fertilized eggs develop without passing through the bipinnaria stage found in many other starfishes.

The Common sunstar feeds on other starfishes, particularly *Asterias rubens*, and when small may attack prey much larger than itself, sometimes causing the attacked starfish to shed the damaged arm and escape rather than be consumed entirely. Sea anemones, Heart urchins, bryozoans, and molluscs may also be eaten, although exactly how this particular species causes bivalves to gape and permit digestion of the soft parts is not fully known. As an active predator it can move relatively quickly, an estimated 14–20 in (35–50 cm) per minute. FAMILY: Solasteridae, ORDER: Spinulosa, CLASS: Asteroidea, PHYLUM: Echinodermata.   E.P.F.R.

SUPERNORMAL STIMULUS, one that is greater than the stimulus normally required to evoke the appropriate response in an animal. Remarkably, a supernormal stimulus is often more effective than the normal, and such

Actinaster planci, one of the sunstars.

stimuli possibly account for some of the unusual things animals do. Experimental tests have shown the Ringed plover *Charadrius alexandrinus*, when given the choice of a normal egg and a model egg with larger, more conspicuous markings, will accept the larger egg to brood. An oystercatcher, *Haematopus ostralagus*, given three eggs, one its own, one a gull's egg, and a dummy egg nearly as large as itself, will try to incubate the large egg.

SURFPERCHES, a family containing principally marine perch-like fishes from the North Pacific and living chiefly in the surf. The most notable feature of this family is that it is one of the very few marine groups of bony fishes that is viviparous, giving birth to live young instead of depositing eggs. This was first definitely confirmed in 1835 and many studies have since been made on these curious fishes. The majority of surfperches are found off the Pacific coasts of North America, but two species, *Ditrema temmincki* and *Neoditrema ransonetti*, live off Japanese coasts. A single species, the Tule perch *Hysterocarpus traski*, is known from freshwater.

One of the best known species is the Shiner surfperch *Cymatogaster aggregata* which is common in the region of San Francisco. The male has the anal fin modi-fied for copulation. The number of young depends on the size of the female and can range from 3 to 60. Few surfperches reach more than 18 in (46 cm) in length. Unlike many viviparous fishes, the eggs contain rather little yolk and the embryos are nourished by a fluid secreted in the ovary. The young are unusual not only in being well-developed at birth but in the case of the males in being sexually mature immediately after birth. Another peculiarity is that although copulation takes place in the breeding season during the summer, fertilization does not seem to occur until the winter, the sperm being stored until that time. In this way one year elapses between copulation and the birth of the young.

The Tule perch would seem to be an ideal species for an aquarium since it lives in freshwater. In fact it has proved almost impossible to keep, perhaps requiring the silt that it finds in rivers for its well-being. FAMILY: Embiotocidae. ORDER: Perciformes, CLASS: Pisces.

SURGEONFISHES, a group of marine fishes characteristic of coral reefs. Their name derives from the little bony keels, often extremely sharp and blade-like, on either side at the base of the tail (i.e. on the caudal peduncle). In some species these little

Surgeonfishes—this one is *Zebrasoma veliferum*—are so named for the sharp knife-like spine at the base of the tailfin, which can be erected for defence.

'knives' are hinged at the rear and can thus be erected to point forwards so that care should be taken when handling live specimens. In the *unicornfish there are several bony keels on each side of the peduncle. The surgeonfishes are deep-bodied and compressed, with small terminal mouths bearing a single row of cropping teeth in each jaw. They feed by scraping algae and other organisms from rocks and coral.

Some variation in colour is found in the surgeonfishes. In the Yellow surgeon *Zebrasoma flavescens* there are yellow and grey-brown colour phases and the Common surgeonfish of the Atlantic *Acanthurus bahianus* has been observed to change when chasing another member of the species, from its normal blue-grey colouring to white anteriorly and dark behind. The Five-banded surgeonfish *A. triostegus,* an Indo-Pacific species that reaches 10 in (25 cm), has a dark, apple-green body with dark brown vertical bars. Also known as the convictfish, it has been involved in cases of fish poisoning. During development, the young surgeonfishes pass through a curious larval or acronurus stage in which the body has vertical ridges and does not closely resemble that of the adult.

In the Indo-Pacific area some of the surgeonfishes are popular as food and are extremely tasty; in fish markets the offending keels on the caudal peduncle are often cut off prior to display. FAMILY: Acanthuridae, ORDER: Perciformes, CLASS: Pisces.

SURICATE *Suricata suricatta*, the alternative name for the *meerkat.

SURINAM TOAD *Pipa pipa,* a tongueless frog of curiously flattened appearance and living wholly in water in the Amazon and Orinoco basins. See Pipidae.

SUSPENSION FEEDING. Many aquatic animals use, as food, particles or creatures which are very small relative to their own size. The 80 ft (24 m) Baleen whale feeds on small crustaceans 2 in (5 cm) in length. It is impractical that this enormous mammal should capture its prey individually. Instead, it concentrates its food by filtering large quantities of seawater passing into its mouth as it swims. The mesh of the horny filter of 'baleen' which hangs in the mouth is the correct size to separate the krill from the water. In this animal we see many of the characteristics of suspension feeding. The Baleen whale is specialized for this method of feeding both structurally and in its behaviour. It has lost the teeth which are present in other whales, which eat larger animals, and it is confined to the surface waters of the Antarctic where the suitable plankton occurs. In common with many, though not all, of the free-living animals which are adapted to suspension feeding, the whale is using its normal locomotion to sample large quantities of water.

The use of filtering mechanisms to obtain food in this way is of rare occurrence amongst vertebrates though it is seen in certain fishes, including the Basking shark, and also in flamingoes. Each of these are isolated genera whose specialized feeding mechanisms do not reflect the general trends of the group to which they belong. It is, in fact, more usual to speak of these large animals as filter-feeders, although the distinction is a fine one. There are, however, whole phyla or large subgroupings in which all or the majority of species obtain their nourishment in this way.

All the sponges feed by removing particles from water passing through their bodies. The particles are engulfed by cells lining the canals and cavities which permeate the whole animal. These animals are sedentary and have to ensure that large quantities of water enter the body for clearance, a problem which does not arise in the active whale.

Sponges use flagella, whip-like extensions of many cells lining their internal channels, to draw water through the numerous pores on the surface of the body and keep it moving through their interior. Abyssal sponges and also the Sea fans, in shallow water gullies, stand in the path of unidirectional currents and remove particles from water brought to them in this way.

Some suspension feeding animals do not actually filter water during feeding. The brittlestars raise two or three of their arms to expose their undersurface to the current. Any particles touching the ventral surface are carried to the mouth. The complex fan of the fanworms is not behaving as a filter when expanded. Water is flushed over a variety of grooves where particles become entangled in a viscous mucus secretion.

Many sedentary animals have internal or external filters, however, which are held in the path of water currents created by themselves. In the bivalves and Sea squirts the external form of the body is modified with inhalant and exhalant siphons for the entry and exit of water. Particles in suspension are separated from the water as it passes through a screen of mucus spread over a perforated pharynx or gill. Whip-like cilia are used for maintaining the water current, applying the mucus filter and subsequently for transporting the particle-laden mucus along grooves to the mouth.

Certain features of this method of obtaining food are automatic, The animals are unable to distinguish between nutritious and inert particles, though the current is often stopped in the presence of toxic substances. Grading of particles occurs in both the fanworms and the bivalves. Only the smaller particles enter the mouth and the larger particles are transported along different pathways for rejection. Blockage is liable to occur in animals with internal filters. General contraction of the body clears water and debris from inside the Sea squirt when a blockage occurs.

Control of the rate of flow of water is not so critical in animals using an external filter within the confines of a tube or burrow. In the bizarre bristleworm *Chaetopterus* and also in the *mudshrimps, several limbs are modified as fans or baffles to push water past the body. Particles are removed by a fine mesh of spines borne on the front limbs in the mudshrimps and by a mucus sieve in *Chaetopterus*. Other bristleworms use a piston-like action of the body wall for irrigation.

The jointed limbs of barnacles form a scoop for removing particles in suspension. This is either held out in moving water or is repeatedly swept through the water.

Suspension feeding is common amongst the smaller free-living crustaceans. Filtration is by means of fine spines on the edges of some or all of the limbs. The synchronized movements of the limbs during locomotion creates currents of water through these filters in the Fairy shrimps, Water fleas and copepods. These animals are of particular importance since they are feeding on the microscopic plants of the plankton and are therefore the first link with the primary producers of the aquatic environments.

In water as on land, the primary source of food is that synthesized by plants. Large attached plants play a relatively small part in the economy of the oceans owing to the absence of light in deep waters, and the microscopic plants of the plankton are the primary source of food in the ocean. Small crustaceans, particularly the cladocerans, consume these in large numbers. Some larger animals including the doliolids and salps also take the living plants, filtering them from a current of water passing through the body. The smallest plant cells are taken by planktonic invertebrate larvae which entangle them in mucus strands associated with cilia on the surface of their body.

Many of the plant cells die before being eaten and are subject to bacterial attack. The products contribute to the particulate matter in suspension in the ocean. Other organic particles or detritus result from bacterial breakdown of dead animals. Material brought down by rivers increases the particulate content of the sea, and waters around Iceland and Greenland receive some from melting icebergs. Animals of coastal and inland waters and of estuaries are subject to run off from the land, although much of the suspension in these areas may be mud or sand arising from agitation of the bottom deposits by wind and tide. It is now realized that the bacteria themselves, together with certain chemicals in suspension, make an important contribution to the nutrition of aquatic animals.   W.A.M.C.

European swallows in a barn, the parent bird clinging to the nest of mud pellets strengthened with grass stems.

SWALLOWS, a distinctive and successful cosmopolitan family of some 78 species of perching birds, many of which are more commonly known as martins. There is, however, no significant difference between 'swallows' and 'martins'. All have long wings and agile flight and feed almost entirely on insects they catch in the air. One species, *Riparia riparia*, is known as the Sand martin in Britain and the Bank swallow in America. They are all rather small birds, varying from $3\frac{3}{4}$–9 in (9.5–22.8 cm) in length, and in a number of species much of this is taken up by the long, forked tail. The plumage is generally dark; black, brown, green, or blue, often with a metallic sheen. Several species show white in the spread tail, and many species are paler on the underside of the body. The neck and legs are short, and the feet small and weak. Swallows perch readily on wires, branches and other vegetation, but due to their leg and foot structure they are clumsy on the ground. In several species the whole of the legs, sometimes even the toes, are feathered.

The general characteristics of the swallows are centred around their adaptations for feeding on the aerial plankton, the insects and other invertebrates which are carried by, or fly weakly in, the air currents. For this reason one of their most outstanding features is the short, broad, and flattened bill which can be opened to a very wide gape forming a highly efficient insect trap. It also acts as a trowel for scooping up mud for nest-building.

Swallows have a world-wide distribution, some individual species being found in both Old and New Worlds. Only the extreme latitudes and some oceanic islands are without one or more species of swallow. Most species are gregarious and all are migratory. In temperate climates especially, birds which depend on the aerial plankton are forced to migrate for that part of the year when the insects on which they feed are not flying. Some of these migrations are of very great length. The European swallow *Hirundo rustica*, for example, may fly 7,000 miles (11,000 km) from northern Europe to South Africa. And, if it survives long enough, it will undertake this journey twice a year.

Swallows – and in particular the European swallow, known in America as the Barn swallow (or in both countries simply as 'swallow') – have long held a special place in the affections of many people. They are attractive in plumage, flight and voice; they are beneficial in that they consume vast numbers of harmful insects; they nest relatively fearlessly in suitable buildings such as barns and outhouses; and in particular they act as harbingers of spring. In many north-temperate countries the arrival of the swallows is welcomed as a sign that the winter is truly past. For swallows can only survive when there is a sufficient supply of flying insects, and these in turn depend on suitably warm weather. The swallow in fact follows the northward movement of the 48°F (9°C) isotherm, and its northern limit is around the 53°F (12°C) July isotherm. The saying that 'one swallow does not make a summer' is derived from the occasional appearance of a single bird too early to find a continuing supply of insects. Such individuals must retire south again, or die.

Occasionally some species of swallows will feed on berries. Tree swallows *Iridoprocne bicolor*, for example, are sometimes caught by an early autumn cold snap in Cape Cod, Massachusetts, and may then be seen feeding on bayberry fruits.

Most species breed more or less colonially. The nest may be made in a hole in a tree or rock face, or even a building; or a tunnel may be excavated in the ground – usually in a bank – with the actual nest perhaps several feet underground; or a mud structure may be built – either cup-shaped or enclosed, with an opening in the side – and placed on a branch, beam, rock surface or fixed to a rock face. Buildings make good substitute cliffs and some species, such as the House martin *Delichon urbica* have taken to applying their mud nests to the walls under the eaves of buildings. In the species in which the nest is made of mud it is common for the female to do the building while the male carries the material. The female also seems to play the major role in incubation. The clutch contains three to seven eggs, according to species, which are white, sometimes speckled. The newly-hatched young are helpless and almost naked, and the developmental period is an extended one as the young must be able to fly well on leaving the nest. The fledgling period may thus be longer than three weeks, both parents feeding the young throughout this period. In spite of the long development some species may rear two or three broods in a season, even in temperate countries. However, at the northern limits of a species' range there may be only time for one brood in the brief period between winter snows.

Three genera of swallows are cosmopolitan in distribution: *Hirundo*, containing 13 species, *Petrochelidon* with ten, and *Riparia* with four. The swallow, itself, is found through most of the Palearctic and Nearctic regions, its original habitat apparently having been steppe country with large grazing animals which would disturb insects on which it could feed. Ten species of *Hirundo* are restricted to Africa. Two of these, the Red-chested swallow *H. lucida* from tropical West Africa, and the Angola swallow *H. angolensis* from Central and East Africa, have been said to be conspecific with *H. rustica*. Another similar species is the Coast swallow *H. tahitica,* which is widely distributed in Southeast Asia and Polynesia. In parts of China and Formosa it is found breeding alongside *H. rustica*. The Welcome swallow of Australia and Tasmania is sometimes regarded as a race of the Coast swallow and sometimes given specific rank as *H. neoxena*. Throughout this genus the nest is an open cup made principally of mud or similar material.

Swallows return from Africa to Europe in spring and each returns precisely to its nesting-place of the previous year.

Swallows gather on telegraph wire as the time for migration grows near.

The genus *Petrochelidon*, contains three species in America, four in Africa, one in Asia and two in Australia. In America the Cliff swallow *P. pyrrhonota* is a well-known bird, breeding from Canada and Alaska, in the north, to Mexico, in the south. It winters in South America. Like other members of the genus it builds a retort-shaped nest attached to cliff faces or buildings.

In the genus *Riparia* a nesting burrow is excavated, usually in steep banks but occasionally in ground which may be almost level. The Sand martin or Bank swallow is another successful holarctic species, being equally well known on both sides of the Atlantic. Two other species of the genus are purely African while another is found in both Africa and Asia.

Seven genera of swallows are found only in the Old World. There are three species of *Delichon*, two of them Asiatic, and the House martin *D. urbica* which is found throughout the Palearctic as far north as the 50°F (10°C) July isotherm. There are a few unusual instances of this species breeding in southern Africa, which must be an example of colonization as a result of migration across the equator. This genus has a noticeable amount of white in the plumage.

The genus *Ptyonoprogne* contains three

species in Africa and Asia controversially distinct from the Crag martin *P. rupestris*, which breeds across the Palearctic. Birds of this group tend to be sedentary rather than migratory. The nests are substantial, open mud cups built in a variety of rocky situations.

Of the genus *Cecropis*, four species are African, one Asian and the other, the Red-rumped swallow *C. daurica*, has a discontinuous distribution across parts of southern Europe, southern Asia, and central Africa. Some authorities do not separate these birds from *Hirundo*, but as all swallows are really rather similar, distinctions can be made on the type of nest built, and in this particular group the nests are flask-shaped with an entrance tunnel up to 12 in (30 cm) long, made of mud, and placed in crevices or on walls or rock faces under an overhang.

The Rough-winged swallows of the genus *Psalidoprocne* comprise a group of African species difficult to classify. One recent revision has suggested that there are five species. These birds live around the edges of forests and in clearings where they hawk for insects in the typical swallow manner. They make their nests in burrows, tunnelling into the banks of streams and even into the walls of pitfall traps dug to catch much bigger animals.

The Grey-rumped swallow *Pseudhirundo griseopyga* is another African species which nests in a burrow, but this bird has the unusual habit of using the burrows of small rodents. These tunnels are generally in fairly level ground and the breeding season is therefore necessarily associated with the dry season.

The remaining Old World genera are *Phedina* with two species in Africa and Madagascar, and *Cheramoeca* with the one species of Black-and-white swallow, *C. leucosternum*, in Australia.

In the New World there are nine genera of swallows not found elsewhere. None of them makes a mud nest, nor do they excavate holes for themselves, but nest in a variety of situations in pre-existing holes. The Tree swallow *Tachycineta bicolor* is a well-known species of the north temperate region breeding from Alaska southwards. It is clear white beneath and a green- or blue-black above. There are five other species in the genus, three of them restricted to South America.

The Rough-winged swallow *Stelgidopteryx ruficollis* not closely related to the above group of Rough-winged swallows, is so-called by reason of the serrations on the web of the outer primary wing feathers. It breeds in a variety of subspecific forms from southern Canada southwards to the Gulf of Mexico.

A particularly well-known American species is the Purple martin *Progne subis*. This is a rather large species in which the male is uniformly blue-black above and below, while the female is light-bellied. Such a distinction between the plumage of the sexes is unusual in swallows. One of the reasons that the Purple martin is well known is the readiness with which it takes to breeding in nesting boxes and other artificial sites. It will breed colonially and may thus be seen inhabiting artificial 'apartment houses'. The custom of hanging gourds on poles for these birds, common in the South, was established before European settlement in the New World.

The Golden swallow *Kalochelidon euchrysea* with green upperparts glossed with blue or bronze, is restricted to Hispaniola and Jamaica where it is largely found in the higher regions in the mountains.

Only one species of swallow has doubtful affinities with the others. This is the African River martin *Pseudochelidon eurystomina* which differs from the other swallows in a number of structural features and is therefore placed in a subfamily of its own. This bird is apparently restricted to one part of the Congo. It is large, with dark plumage and red bill and eyes. It nests in large colonies in burrows in the sandy shoals exposed in the river beds during the dry season. The rainy season is spent in the coastal marshes.

In general the swallows form one of the most highly-regarded of bird groups. Some of the reasons for this esteem have already been mentioned, but we may also note that their impressive migrations have long attracted the attention of naturalists. In fact their comings and goings, before the facts of migration were settled, did much to stimulate enquiry into the subject.

The great English naturalist Gilbert White, in the middle 18th century, did excellent work on the British species of the family, yet he found difficulty in considering the swallow robust enough to undertake the journey to South Africa and back. He suspected the occurrence of migration but could not believe it. Since then we have learned much of the amazing powers of flight of these seemingly frail birds, but there is still much to be discovered concerning their travels and distribution. FAMILY: Hirundinidae, ORDER: Passeriformes, CLASS: Aves.

P.M.D.

Swamp deer, a species in danger of extinction that has been introduced to parks in various parts of the world.

SWALLOW CONGLOBULATIONS. It was once widely believed that swallows spent the winter asleep at the bottom of ponds. Dr Johnson, famous for his English dictionary and weighty pronouncements, stated that 'a number of them (swallows) conglobulate together, by flying round and round, and then all in a heap throw themselves under water'. Johnson lived in the latter half of the 18th century and one of his contemporaries, J. L. Frisch tied dyed threads to the legs of swallows. As they appeared the following spring with the dye still visible they could not have spent the winter under water.

SWALLOW-TANAGER *Tersina viridis*, sparrow-sized bright bird of Central and South America. It is the only species in the family Tersinidae. The male is largely turquoise blue, but the face and throat are black, the flanks barred with black and the lower underparts are white. What is blue in the male is green in the female. The bill is short.

The species has a wide distribution, from Panama south through Central America to the tropical areas of South America. They are gregarious birds which live in trees. They nest in holes in the ground but also in holes in trees. The nest itself is made of fine stems and grass. They lay two to four eggs which are incubated by the female. The nestlings are fed by both parents. Adults feed on insects, which are often captured in flight, and on fruit. FAMILY: Tersinidae, ORDER: Passeriformes, CLASS: Aves.

SWAMMERDAM, J., 1637–1680, Dutch naturalist and invertebrate anatomist. Although qualified in medicine he devoted his short life to the study of natural history and made such skilled micro-dissections and meticulous observations that his work was to remain unsurpassed for over 100 years. He described the life-histories of many insects and classified them according to their different kinds of development, thus laying the foundations of modern entomology. His anatomical work on both invertebrates and vertebrates was outstanding. For example, he described the mammalian ovarian follicles and the valves of the lymphatic system, as well as the general anatomy of such animals as the bee, the mayfly and the frog, and he showed that muscles do not alter their size during contraction.

SWAMP DEER *Cervus duvauceli*, included among the endangered species of deer having only a limited distribution in eastern and northern India, and in southern Nepal and Assam. In some parts of India it is known as gond, whilst in others as

barasingha, a name which is also used to describe the hangul or Kashmir deer. There are two subspecies: *C. d. duvauceli* in the area north of the Ganges and *C. d. branderi* in the central parts of India.

They stand about 47–49 in (119–124 cm) high at the shoulder and are generally reddish-brown in colour, while the calves are spotted at birth. There is considerable variation in the pattern of the antlers, which usually bear 10 to 15 points, or even more, the majority of which project above the main beam from about two-thirds of the way up. During growth the antlers are covered with a beautiful red-coloured velvet.

During the rut, which, in India, generally takes place about the end of the year, each stag collects a harem of hinds in much the same way as does the European Red deer stag. The stags utter a peculiar braying sound comparable to that of a donkey.

Whilst the northern race is a dweller of swamp lands, the favourite habitats of the southern race are large grassy plains or maidans on which the deer can graze and rest, preferring to live in, or on the edge of, these plains than to penetrate far into the jungle-clad hills. Whilst resting the deer are constantly attended by the Indian mynah birds which search for ticks in their coats.

Swamp deer from India have been introduced to a few parks in other parts of the world—notably to Woburn in England. FAMILY: Cervidae, ORDER: Artiodactyla, CLASS: Mammalia.   C.P.G.

SWAMP EELS, fishes of fresh and brackish waters of Central and South America, West Africa, Southeast Asia and Australia, resembling eels but belonging to a separate order of uncertain affinities. The body is long and slender, the pectoral and pelvic fins are absent, and the dorsal and anal fins are reduced to fleshy ridges. Swamp eels are frequently found in small, swampy streams and are able to breathe air direct from the atmosphere. Species such as the Rice eel *Monopterus albus* are able to survive the dry season in holes in the mud. The gills are often very reduced and the opening to the gill chamber is under the throat (there is only one opening in *M. albus*). The Rice eel is found from northern China to Malaya and grows to about 3 ft (1 m) long. The naked skin is brownish, spotted with dark brown and there is a black line extending from the snout to the eye. It hides by day but comes out at night to feed on crustaceans and fishes. It is kept by aquarists and its breeding habits have been studied. The male builds a loose *Bubble nest which he guards against predators when the eggs have been laid.

In the marine synbranchid *Macrotrema caligans*, found in the Malayan peninsula, the gills are normal and there is a single long gill opening.

The cuchia *Amphipnous cuchia* from India is placed in a separate family, Amphipnoidae. It has two lung-like sacs opening from the gill chamber and extending under the skin of the nape and a little behind this, where they can be seen as distinct bulges; the gills on the other hand, are very much reduced. It spends a large part of its time out of water wriggling in wet grass and mud in its search for food. During the dry season it *aestivates in the mud.

Typhlosynbranchus, family Synbranchidae, is a blind cave dwelling member of this group. FAMILIES: Synbranchidae and Amphipnoidae, ORDER: Synbranchiformes, CLASS: Pisces.

SWANS, a small group of large, long-necked aquatic birds in the order Anseriformes, which also includes the ducks and geese. The swans are closely related to many geese and are usually put with them in the tribe Anserini. There are only eight species, but their size and, at times, aggressiveness assured them of a place in the economy and folk-lore of man in earlier times. Of the eight species, seven are placed in the genus *Cygnus*. The remaining one, the Coscoroba swan *Coscoroba coscoroba,* may not be a true swan for it has characteristics which suggest that it provides a link between the swans and geese and another group, the Whistling ducks. The Coscoroba, a white bird with black wing-tips, has a shorter neck than the other swans, pink legs and feet and a bright red bill. It breeds in the southern part of South America and migrates north to warmer areas in the southern winter. It derives its name from its call.

Two of the seven species of *Cygnus* are found in the southern hemisphere. The Black swan *C. atratus* is naturally confined to Australia, though it has been introduced elsewhere and now flourishes in New Zealand. It is black with white primaries and a red bill. The Black-necked swan *C. melanocorypha* comes from southern parts of South America. It is, as its name suggests, a white bird with a black neck and head. It has a red bill and knob and is the smallest of the genus. The other five species are all white in adult plumage, though they have bills of different colours, and are all found in the northern hemisphere.

The Trumpeter swan *C. buccinator* breeds in northwestern USA and southwestern Canada. Largely resident, it has been close to extinction but strict protection has enabled it to increase in numbers to its present level of around 1,500 birds. The Whistling swan *C. columbianus* breeds in the high Arctic of western Canada and Alaska and winters largely on the eastern and western seaboard of the United States. Bewick's swan *C. bewickii* also breeds in the high Arctic, across Russia and Siberia, and migrates south for

The Black-necked swan of South America and the Australian Black swan artificially join company.

mists have called them four species, others have called them two, considering the Trumpeter and Whistling swans to be geographical replacements of the Whooper and Bewick's swans respectively. Yet a third view is that there are three species: the Whistling being grouped with the Bewick's, but the Trumpeter and Whooper kept as separate species. The Trumpeter is the only one of the four species which is largely resident. The actual noise of a swan's call is affected by the shape of its windpipe, and the shape of the latter and its route through the breastbone is not only complicated but quite different in the Trumpeter and Whooper swans, whereas there are no such differences between the Whistling and Bewick's swans.

The calls of the swans are very variable, being loud and distinctive in the four species just mentioned and softer in the other three. The so-called 'Mute' swan emits quite a series of hisses and grunts. This species also makes a distinctive noise in flight, a sighing whistle, produced by the wings on the downstroke. A similar noise is made by the Black and Black-necked swans.

All the swans are large and the Mute, Trumpeter and Whooper swans at about 35 lb (16 kg) approach the upper weight limit for flying birds. Consequently they have some difficulty in getting airborne. They may need long 'runs' over land or water to get off and they greatly prefer to land on water so as to reduce the shock to the 'undercarriage'—the legs. Once airborne they fly powerfully, with their necks outstretched. The migrant species may fly long distances at a time. Although strong fliers, they are poor at manoeuvring in flight; again a consequence of their large size. Because of this the Mute swan suffers high mortality from collisions with objects, especially overhead cables. Such cables, so common in western Europe, are not easily seen from a distance, especially if there is any mist or fog. Once close the swan is unable to climb or drop sufficiently quickly to avoid them. Cables are the most common cause of death for the Mute swan in southern and central England and they may cause sufficient deaths to reduce the numbers of swans below that which the rivers could support.

All species are vegetarians and breeding occurs on freshwater, as a rule, though some may spend other seasons on salt water. Recently the Mute swan has been increasing by breeding on the coasts in the brackish water of the Baltic and the breeding colony at Abbotsbury in Dorset is also on slightly brackish water. Feeding may be by grazing on grass away from water or by up-ending to reach aquatic vegetation. Since swans only very rarely dive, and then not for food, they are restricted to areas of shallow water, except for roosting.

the winter, many then being seen in Europe. The Whooper swan *C. cygnus* breeds largely to the south of the Bewick's breeding areas and in Iceland. A few pairs breed as far south as Scotland, but most of these also have to migrate to milder areas to the south for the winter—the time when they can be seen most easily in Britain. The last species, the Mute swan *C. olor*, breeds largely south of the Whooper. It is mainly resident in Europe, but in Asia and in the cooler parts of Europe it may have to leave for the winter. The natural range of this last species is not so well known since much of its present distribution may be due to man's interference. From the Romans onwards the birds have been moved around to establish new stocks. They were much valued for food and from the 13th to the 18th century all swans in Britain were the property of the Crown and the ownership of herds under licence was a much valued possession. During this time the complex series of bill markings, which identified ownership, evolved. This has now largely ceased though the Vintners and Dyers Companies still retain the right to mark the birds on the lower

reaches of the Thames. There has even been discussion as to whether this species is a true member of the British avifauna since it may not have bred here before its introduction by the Romans.

The Mute swan has a red bill when adult, the Whooper and Bewick's swans both have black and yellow bills, while the Trumpeter's is black and the Whistling swan's black with or without a small yellow spot. The swans in both 'pairs' of species (Whooper and Bewick's; Trumpeter and Whistling) are thus superficially similar. In fact the Bewick's swan, named *Cygnus bewickii* in honour of the great illustrator of birds, Thomas Bewick, was only recognized as a separate species and named by Yarrell in 1830, some 70 years after the Whooper had been scientifically described and named. Not only are the two pairs of swans alike, but taxonomists are not all in agreement as to how many species there are. The Whooper and Bewick are very similar to the Trumpeter and Whistling swans of the New World. In both pairs there is a large (Whooper, Trumpeter) and a small (Bewick's, Whistling) bird. Some taxono-

Opposite: mute swans at their nest among reeds.

All species may gather into flocks outside the breeding season, but most normally breed in pairs that are isolated from one another. The most notable exception to this is the Australian Black swan which breeds in colonies—sometimes several thousand pairs in a single colony. The Mute swan by way of contrast is normally highly territorial and the male defends his territory vigorously against intruders and this includes his own young of the previous year once spring arrives. In spite of this aggressive behaviour, which usually results in the pairs being separated by 1 mile (1·6 km), or more, even on large rivers, the Mute swan may nest much more densely under certain conditions. In towns, for example, where the birds are regularly fed, the territories may be reduced to 60–90 ft (18–27 m) though they are still defended aggressively. The aggressive behaviour of the males may be confined to the nest-site alone in places where the Mute swan nests colonially. The only site in Britain where this occurs is at the Abbotsbury Swannery in Dorset where swans have nested close to one another for some 600 years; exceptionally over 100 pairs have nested in this colony. While such behaviour is rare and the reasons for it are not understood, this colony is not unique as there are others in Denmark and Poland.

All species of swans nest near to the water and make a large nest of rushes or aquatic vegetation. Clutch size is usually about four to seven eggs, though single Mute swans have been recorded as laying up to 12 eggs. The arctic breeding Whistling and Bewick's swans lay clutches at the lower end of this range and four eggs is probably the average. The eggs are large—those of the larger species usually weigh about $\frac{3}{4}$ lb (0·3 kg)—and the female normally lays an egg every other day. Incubation starts when the clutch is nearly complete and takes about four weeks in the smaller species, five weeks in the larger ones, and five and a half in the Black swan. The female does most of the incubation, but the male takes over while his mate goes to feed. While hatching the female stays on the eggs and the young, when dry, are taken into the water and guarded by the male. The young hatch with an unusually large amount of the egg-yolk still unabsorbed, up to 25% of the original yolk being stored inside the newly hatched chick. In the Mute swan, it seems that this provides a valuable source of nourishment for the young bird since it can live without any other food for a week or ten days. The young can fly after about four or five months.

The downy young, called cygnets, are uniform white or light grey in all species when newly hatched, except for the Coscoroba cygnets which are strongly patterned with black. They moult into a plumage of brown feathers and do not acquire the adult colour until one or two years old. The annual moult takes place after breeding, when all the flight feathers are lost simultaneously and the birds are flightless. In the Mute swan the female moults first and the male not until the female is able to fly again so that one of the pair is always able to fly. Mute swans do not usually breed until about four years old, though exceptionally birds may breed at two and breeding three-year olds are not uncommon. FAMILY: Anatidae, ORDER: Anseriformes, CLASS: Aves.   C.M.P.

SWEETLIPS, perch-like marine fishes belonging to the genus *Plectorhynchus,* and deriving their common name from their thick and rather luscious lips. The sweetlips are found commonly in the Indo-Pacific region. They have fairly deep bodies, a small mouth with conical teeth, and the spiny and soft portions of the dorsal fin are joined by a membrane. They grow to about 25 in (64 cm) and many are very strikingly coloured. In *Plectorhynchus chaetodonticeps* the body is brown with large white spots and bars. *P. golmani* has diagonal blue stripes on a silvery body, while the fins are yellow with blue spots. In some species, however, the young are quite different from the adults in colour, a situation which is not uncommon in reef-dwelling species and which in the past has often led zoologists to describe the young and the adults as two different species. FAMILY: Pomadasyidae, ORDER: Perciformes, CLASS: Pisces.

Opposite: sweetlips *Plectorhynchus chaetodonticeps*, a reef fish of tropical Indo-Pacific seas.

Below: mute swan with cygnets.

All swifts are similar in appearance, and are often confused with swallows which, however, are not related and are placed in the order Passeriformes. There are nearly 80 species of swifts distributed throughout the major land masses of the world, excepting Antarctica and Australia where they occur only in the northernmost areas. The majority of species live in the warmer parts of the world and although several breed in temperate regions (as far north as Alaska, Finland and northern Russia) they do not penetrate far beyond the tree-line, and they migrate to the tropics for the winter.

There are two families of swifts, the Apodidae and the Crested swifts, Hemiprocnidae. The species of the latter family occur in Southeast Asia and the western Pacific. They are less aerial than the other swifts, spending much time perched in trees like large swallows.

The Apodidae is divided into two groups. The genera *Chaetura* (Spine-tailed swifts), *Collocalia* (Cave swiftlets) and *Cypseloides* (including the North American Black swift) form one group. These all have small, stiff spiny projections at the tips of their tail feathers—hence the names spine-tailed or needle-tailed which are applied to some of them. The other group consists of the genus *Apus*, which includes the four species of swifts which breed in Europe, and several smaller genera.

The sexes are similar in all species and the newly fledged young are like the adults. Breeding normally takes place in colonies (as is often the case with the Common swift in Europe) or in single pairs. In the Great Cave at Niah, Sarawak, 2 million pairs of *Collocalia maxima* breed in a single colony. Although there is little information, there is probably a period of several years immaturity. The Common swift probably does not breed until three or four years old.

All species glue the nest structure together with their own saliva. In some species, especially *Collocalia*, the nest is made almost entirely of saliva and the nests are harvested to form the basis of 'birds-nest-soup'. In those species where other materials are combined with the saliva, the materials are normally small leaves, tiny twigs broken from trees and other objects blown about by the wind, which are always collected in flight. The Common swift frequently uses the winged seeds of the elm that are shed at nest-building time and even wind-blown bus tickets are acceptable.

The form and position of the nest differs in different species. Many species are hole-nesters which originally used hollow trees or cliffs, but are now often found in or on buildings. The nest may be a simple cup-shaped structure resting on a ledge, as in the European Common swift and Alpine swift *Apus melba,* or it may be a platform projecting from a vertical face. In the latter

SWIFTLET, the name usually reserved for birds of about 20 species of the genus *Collocalia*—Cave swiftlets distributed through Southeast Asia and parts of the western Pacific. Some nest in huge colonies in caves. The nests of some are used as the basis of 'birds-nest-soup'. Some species find the way to their nests by echolocation in a manner similar to that used by bats. See swifts. FAMILY: Apodidae, ORDER: Apodiformes, CLASS: Aves.

SWIFTS, small, fast flying birds with an almost world-wide distribution. They share the order Apodiformes with the hummingbirds.

Usually they are placed in the suborder Apodi and the hummingbirds in the Trochili, but some authors consider the similarities between the two groups as being due to convergent evolution (i.e. evolution of the same modifications by animals of different groups because both animals live in the same way) and so place them in different orders. Both hummingbirds and swifts are striking in aerial behaviour, although the modes of flight are very different. Both groups have very small feet (hence the name Apodiformes—'no

feet') and legs. Another shared characteristic not shown by any other bird is the extremely short humerus (upper arm), short ulna (lower arm) and extended hand bones. In all birds the major flight feathers are attached to the ulna and the hand, but the swifts and hummingbirds have a peculiar wing in which the hand feathers (primaries) predominate and only a small area is taken up by the feathers in the inner part of the wing (secondaries).

The wing of a swift is long and very narrow so they are extremely fast fliers and are amongst the most aerial of all birds. They catch their food on the wing and at least one species spends the night on the wing. They have small weak bills, but large wide gapes with which they catch insects. The birds are very streamlined, even the eyes being slightly sunk into the side of the head. It is often said that they are unable to take off from flat ground (due to their very short legs and high stalling speed), but this only applies to weak or injured birds (and most grounded birds are sick or injured). However, the European Common swift *Apus apus* is unable to hover and cannot fly for long in small circles. Swifts are poor at manoeuvring and need open spaces for flying.

case the nest must be quite strong since it has to support the weight of at least one adult and several small young.

The edible nests of the Cave swiftlets are of this form and so is the nest of the Chimney swift of North America *Chaetura pelagica* which, as the name suggests, commonly nests in chimneys. One or two species of the genus *Cypseloides* build their nests in caves behind waterfalls, often actually flying through the falling water to reach the nest-site. One *Panyptila* species builds a nest attached to a rock face with a long hanging tube, 2 ft (0·6 m) in length. The entrance is at the bottom of the tube up which the birds have to climb to the nest at the top. One of the Palm swifts, a species of *Cypsiurus,* builds a tiny projection from a hanging palm leaf as its nest. This is so frail and the leaves wave around so much in the wind that the single egg is glued on to the nest with saliva and the bird hangs vertically on to the palm leaf with its belly touching the egg to incubate it. This is one of the only species of bird in which the egg is not turned frequently during the course of incubation. The Crested swifts (Hemiprocnidae) balance their single egg in a crack on a small twig and sit over it, one foot holding the twig on either side of the egg. They too may not turn their egg.

The breeding biology of most of the group is not well known though it seems to be similar in most species. The Common and Alpine swifts of Europe and the Chimney swift of North America are the best known species. Copulation may occur at the nest-site, but at least in some species can also take place when the birds are on the wing. All species lay white, rather elongated eggs and the clutches are small, usually one, two or three, though up to six eggs are laid in a few species. Although the eggs are not very large for the size of the bird, they are usually laid at intervals of two days (most birds of this size lay their eggs at daily intervals). When its food is short in cold weather, the European Common swift lays two instead of three eggs and the interval between the laying is three instead of two days.

The incubation period, about 19–20 days, is long for such small birds. The fledging period is unusually variable and is dependent on the weather which affects the availability of the food. The Common swift young leave the nest at any time between five weeks and eight weeks after hatching. The young of many of the species that build nests which project from a vertical face leave their nests when only partly grown and hang on to the surface beside the nest. Presumably this reduces the chance of the nest collapsing under the weight.

Common swift of Europe: swifts seldom land on the ground, they sometimes cling to vertical walls, and most of their lives they spend on the wing.

In the European Common swift the young migrate immediately after leaving the nest, finding their way without their parents. They moult during the winter in Africa. In another European species, the Alpine swift, the birds moult in Europe and then migrate to Africa, leaving Europe much later than the Common swift. The American Chimney swift is unusual in that it migrates in large flocks which may roost together in a single chimney; sometimes a 'favoured' chimney will be used in successive years. The European Common swift is known to spend the night on the wing under certain conditions, the birds ascending to several thousand feet at dusk and also moving out to sea if they are near the coast. These movements can be clearly seen on a radar screen. It seems likely that many of the immature birds spend most, if not all, of the nights in the summer on the wing; certainly many of them move several hundred miles to avoid areas of depression (where the weather is poor and causing feeding to be poor) and cannot, therefore, return to the same roosting-site each night. Indeed since the birds spend the winter in areas of Africa where it may be dangerous to roost (e.g. on trees in the Congo where there are many predators) it is by no means impossible that the birds actually never land in Africa. If so, then it is the only species of bird to be able to go without sleep—at least in the usually accepted sense.

Swifts have two other abilities which are unusual in birds. Some are known to be able to become torpid in cold weather (to be able to lower their body temperature and 'tick over' very slowly as in hibernation). The young of several species have been known to do this during periods of bad weather when food is short. In winter in California even the adults of the White-throated swift are known to become torpid during periods of bad weather. Torpidity, in birds, is otherwise only known in the nightjars and hummingbirds, two groups closely related to the swifts.

Some of the Cave swiftlets *Collocalia* spp, nest on the walls of large caves, often in total darkness. They find their way to and from their nests and avoid collision with one another by echolocation, rather as bats do. The birds utter a series of clicks which rebound off any object in their path, the echo then being heard by the bird. The method is not exactly the same as that used by bats since the wavelength of the sounds emitted are very much lower, being easily audible to humans. The speed required to 'process' the information coming from such echoes shows that the birds can measure the time interval between sounds very much more finely than can humans. Only one other bird, the oilbird *Steatornis caripensis* from northeastern South America, is known to use echolocation. It is a nightjar—closely related to the swifts.
FAMILIES: Apodidae and Hemiprocnidae, ORDER: Apodiformes, CLASS: Aves. C.M.P.

SWIFT-NEST SOUP. The nests of the Cave swiftlets have been used for hundreds of years to make birds' nest soup. The vital ingredient is the dried saliva which has been shown to have virtually no food value and, by itself, little taste. It is, however, highly appreciated in soups and mixed with strongly tasting seasoning and sauces. It was also thought to be an aphrodisiac.

The nests were collected by knocking them down with rods. This could be a hazardous business as the caves where the swiftlets nested are often very high and the nests could only be reached by climbing specially placed poles, often of great length. Nevertheless it was very profitable, the pure saliva nests bringing more money than those with feathers or vegetation mixed with the saliva which had to be removed. In Sarawak, collection was controlled by the museum, who issued special licences. Old nests were inedible but if new ones were taken, the swiftlets were able readily to replace them. The industry is now failing because falling prices and an improved standard of living make the risks less worthwhile.

SWIFTS' DEEP SLEEP. The first good documentary evidence that swifts can become torpid was in a letter, dated 1767, written by Gilbert White of Selborne. He tells of a friend who was watching an old church tower being dismantled early one spring. Two swifts were found among the rubble, apparently dead, but they revived when brought near a fire. Unfortunately Gilbert White's friend was too zealous in his care of the swifts and they were suffocated by smoke. Since then there have been sporadic reports of apparent hibernation by swifts. In 1913 W. C. Hanna, an American naturalist, found White-throated swifts in rock crevices during a severe winter in California. He took some indoors where they revived.

SWIMBLADDER, also known as gas- or airbladder, a silvery gas-filled sac lying along the top of a fish's body cavity just below the vertebral column. A swimbladder is absent in sharks but is present in most bony fishes. It has been secondarily lost in some groups. In the more primitive bony fishes the swimbladder is connected by a narrow tube to the throat (e.g. in the herring) but in the advanced fishes (e.g. perch) this duct closes and disappears at an early stage in the life-history. Many fishes in which the swimbladder is closed swallow air when young to fill the swimbladder before the duct degenerates. Perch fry, for example, if prevented from reaching the surface, are unable to fill the swimbladder. The primary function of the swimbladder in modern fishes is to give

buoyancy so that they can use their fins for purposes other than merely preventing themselves sinking to the bottom (see fins).

The possession of a swimbladder presents some difficulties to fishes that migrate to and from deeper water. Since the pressure of water decreases as the fish rises to the surface, the volume of the swimbladder increases correspondingly. In a fish rising from considerable depths the swimbladder would soon displace all the other internal organs if there were no means of preventing this. In fishes in which the swimbladder still connects to the throat through a ductus pneumaticus the excess gas can be allowed to escape quite simply. In fishes without a duct the volume of gas is varied by absorption or secretion of gas, through the blood vessels of the oval gland and the gas gland respectively. Neither organ is found in fishes with a duct.

The centre of buoyancy is usually below the centre of gravity so that if the fish leans to one side it will tend to turn upside down. In addition, any upward movement of the fish will tend to expand the swimbladder, making the fish even more buoyant. For these reasons, the fins are rarely still but are constantly engaged in slight correcting movements.

The swimbladder has been lost secondarily in a number of bony fishes, including some deep-sea forms. It is absent in the large ocean-living tuna-like fishes, but the large quantities of oil in the flesh help to provide buoyancy. In sharks the huge oily liver serves the same purpose.

The swimbladder evolved from the lungs found in primitive fishes (see air-breathing fishes) and in modern lungfishes is now only secondarily adapted for breathing air. It is also used as a resonator in some fishes in *sound production.

SWORDFISH *Xiphias gladius*, a large oceanic fish with the snout produced into a powerful, flattened sword. Swordfishes are worldwide, mainly in tropical oceans but also entering temperate waters. They have been recorded off the coasts of northern Europe and occasionally stray as far as Iceland. Rather solitary fishes, they grow to a weight of 1,500 lb (675 kg) and are chiefly found in open waters often at the surface with the high but short dorsal fin cleaving the water like the dorsal fin of a shark. Where common they are exploited commercially, usually being caught by harpoon, and are also much sought after by anglers. Swordfish feed on fishes and squids and examination of their stomach contents shows they also penetrate to depths and feed on deep-sea fishes.

The 'sword' is reputed to be used to thrash amongst shoals of fishes, the swordfish feeding at leisure on the injured fishes. The fish has been known since ancient times both

Male swordtail with young females. This male started life as a female and, after giving birth to several broods, underwent a change of sex and became a fully functional male.

because of its size and because of instances when it has rammed wooden vessels. In the British Museum (Natural History) is preserved a piece of timber from a ship that has been penetrated to a depth of 22 in (56 cm) by the sword of a swordfish. It was also reported that HMS *Dreadnought* was punctured by a swordfish on its return voyage from Ceylon to London, the sword passing right through the copper sheathing of the hull. Swords are occasionally found broken off and embedded in the blubber of whales and it has been suggested that swordfishes mistake ships for whales. It is possible, however, that the swordfish, a fast and powerful swimmer of the open seas, credited with speeds up to 60 mph (96 kmph) has on occasions been unable to divert its course in time to prevent a collision. FAMILY: Xephiidae, ORDER: Perciformes, CLASS: Pisces.

SWORDFISH ATTACKS SUBMARINE.
While swordfishes usually swim near the surface, it is known that they sometimes hunt in deep water because deep-sea fish have been found in their stomachs. Direct evidence has now been provided by the research submarine *Alvin*. While surveying the seabed at a depth of 1,800 ft (600 m) off Georgia, USA it was attacked by a 200 lb (90 kg) swordfish that pierced a joint in the external hull. The fish was unable to extricate itself and was carried to the surface with the *Alvin*.

SWORDTAIL *Xiphophorus helleri,* a live-bearing cyprinodont fish from Mexico and Guatemala. The lower caudal fin rays in the male are prolonged into a 'sword', which is quite soft and used in sexual display. The swordtail has many remarkable features which make it a most instructive aquarium fish. In some instances the female, having given birth to up to 100 young, changes into a male, losing her dark 'pregnancy mark' as the anal fin changes shape and the male sword develops. Such males, once the transformation has been completed, are fully capable of fathering another 100 or so young. In some strains up to 30% of the females change sex. The change from male to female has never been recorded.

In the wild the swordtail is the 'green sword', but the species is variable. A cross with a reddish individual of the closely related species *X. montezumae* (the Montezuma sword) has produced the Red swordtail. A cross with a Wagtail platy has produced the Wagtail sword. FAMILY: Poeciliidae, ORDER: Atheriniformes, CLASS: Pisces.

SYMBIONTS AND SYMBIOSIS. There is much confusion over the use of the term symbiosis. The word was first coined by De Barry in 1879 to mean merely 'the living together' of organisms of different species, but the term has often been used in a more specific sense to indicate only those relationships in which mutual benefit is gained by

both participants. It seems preferable to retain the general sense of the word as suggested by Cheng (1967) and to use 'symbiosis' as a broad ecological term covering all kinds of heterospecific associations which can be grouped under the sub-headings commensalism, mutualism and phoresis. The general term 'symbiosis' can then still be used in the many cases where the relationship between two organisms is not fully understood and therefore cannot be defined further.

'Commensalism' literally means 'eating at the same table' and implies an external superficial association between two organisms which are largely physiologically independent of one another. Examples of commensalism are the association of the remora or suckerfishes with sharks and the association of the oligochaete annelid *Chaetogaster* with freshwater snails, the oligochaete living in the shell of the snail and scavenging food particles. The brightly coloured coral fishes which live within the stinging tentacles of coral polyps, thereby obtaining protection against predators, can also be considered as commensals. Another well-known example is given by the relationship between certain species of Sea anemones and Hermit crabs. The anemone lives on the mollusc shell occupied by the Hermit crab, thus giving protection against predators. In return the anemone benefits from scraps of feed caught and scattered by the crab. Although the relationship between the anemone *Calliactis parasitica* and the Hermit crab *Pagurus bernhardi* is truly commensal the relationship between the anemone *Adamsia palliata* and *Eupagurus pridauxi* is a much more obligatory one and in fact in the latter case neither the anemone nor the crab can survive alone. This, therefore, seems to have evolved into another kind of relationship called 'mutualism'.

'Mutualism' describes a far more intimate kind of relationship where the mutualist and the host are dependent on one another usually because of some metabolic exchange between the two. This kind of relationship may verge on parasitism although the latter involves only a unilateral advantage. For instance, termites feed on wood but are unable to digest the wood themselves and are completely dependent on the presence in their hind-gut of certain characteristic flagellate protozoans which do this for them. The flagellates produce cellulases which break down the wood and the termites then live on the flagellates. An analogous situation occurs in the gut of certain herbivorous mammals, notably the ruminants, which depend on a flora and fauna of cellulase-producing bacteria and ciliates to digest the plant material they eat. Other examples of mutualistic endosymbiosis occur in the relationships of algae with the tissues of certain aquatic invertebrates. Marine invertebrates tend to have yellow algae or zooxanthellae and fresh water forms have green algae or zoochlorellae. Examples of marine animals having algae in their tissues are the coelenterate corals and some anemones, the flatworm *Convoluta,* the polychaete annelid *Eunice gigantea* and the Giant clam *Tridacna.* There is some evidence that metabolic exchanges occur both between the symbiotic algae and host cells and also in the other direction. For instance, work using radioactively labelled carbon compounds has shown that substances such as glycerol produced by the algae in photosynthesis can be taken up by cells of the host anemone. In most cases it seems unlikely that photosynthetic products are of significant use to the anemone because many are active carnivores; however, it is possible that the algae provide an accessory food reserve which can be drawn upon in times of stress. It has been found that the green freshwater *Chlorohydra viridissima* can withstand starvation better than albinos. It is also possible that algae can produce co-enzymes, vitamins or hormone-like trace substances which are of use to the polyps.

In corals the symbiotic algae have been shown to assist in the formation of the calcareous skeleton since corals with zooxanthellae grow faster than those without them or than those kept in darkness. Skeleton formation involves uptake of calcium and bicarbonate ions from seawater; these combine in the tissues of the coral to form insoluble calcium carbonate which forms the skeleton, plus carbon dioxide and water. The algae 'mop up' excess carbon dioxide and use it for photosynthesis, thus displacing the equilibrium in a favourable direction for renewed combination of calcium and bicarbonate. Recent evidence suggests that certain marine, slug-like saccoglossid molluscs can store free chloroplasts in their tissues which may be mutualists. The chloroplasts are obtained from the alga *Codium* on which the Sea slugs feed by piercing the cell walls. More evidence of biochemical exchanges between the cells of the Sea slug and the free chloroplasts is required, however, before a truly mutualistic relationship can be established. The chloroplasts could have only a temporary existence within the mollusc cells and might serve mainly to camouflage the vulnerable soft-bodied Sea slugs. There is a theory that the chloroplasts of all higher green plants originated as a symbiotic relationship between the colourless ancestors of these plants and algae. The relationship between the cytoplasm of modern plants and the chloroplasts is, however, a very intimate one and has transcended symbiosis as such. The interdependence between symbiont and partner may be so great that direct transmission to the offspring occurs. The eggs of

Hermit crabs live in the empty shells of whelks and other gastropod molluscs. This one, *Pagurus prideauxi,* lives in symbiosis with the Cloak anemone *Adamsia palliata,* which wraps itself round the shell.

Chlorohydra viridissima are naturally contaminated with zoochlorellae so that the infection is inherited. Insects, such as aphids feeding on plant juices, have special organs termed mycetomes which contain yeasts and are situated near the ovaries in the body cavity. Aphids extract a great deal of sugar from the plants on which they feed and give out excess in the form of honeydew. It seems that the function of the yeasts might be to provide enzymes to facilitate sugar digestion. These yeasts penetrate the ovaries of the aphids and are transmitted in the eggs. Where endosymbionts are not inherited some active behavioural process may occur to ensure that the symbiont is not lost. Thus the Leaf ants which cultivate a fungus garden on leaf fragments take bundles of fungus with them when swarming, these being carried in hypopharyngeal pockets. Similarly in insects such as the Flour weevil which depend on symbiotic yeasts to provide B vitamins lacking in their diet the newly hatched larvae normally acquire symbionts by eating the egg shell which is contaminated with them. Young termites acquire their symbiotic flagellates by ingesting the contaminated faeces of older termites. Indeed, this process has to be repeated throughout larval life after moults because defaunation occurs as the lining of the hind-gut is shed with the rest of the 'skin'.

'Phoresis' resembles commensalism more than mutualism in that it is a loose non-obligatory kind of relationship. It differs from commensalism in that the participants do not share food. The term phoresis is often used when one organism obtains shelter and is transported around by another organism or at least gains an attachment site from the participant. One example is a fish *Fierasfer* which lives internally in the respiratory tree of holothurian Sea cucumbers. The fish is very vulnerable and if kept in a tank with other fishes, but without the holothurian, is preyed upon. Living in association with the holothurian it is transported from place to place in safety. Similarly the resistant daur larvae of certain soil nematodes may become associated with beetles for a period in their life-history and thus become distributed over a wide area. Increasing dependence on the beetle during the phoretic phase has, it seems, led to parasitism in some of these rhabditiform nematodes.   K.L.

SYMPATRIC AND ALLOPATRIC SPECIES. Sympatric species are those species or subspecies having the same geographical range, or having overlapping ranges, but which do not crossbreed under the conditions of their natural environment.

Allopatric species, or subspecies, are those having geographical ranges which do not overlap with one another, so that crossbreeding has been prevented.

The geographical isolation of a population is probably the major factor leading to the formation of new species. Changes in the isolated population, sufficient to allow us to regard it as a new subspecies or species, may be due to two main factors: genetic drift and natural selection. The theory of genetic drift states that in populations of less than 100 breeding animals, mutations with no adaptive significance can become established in the gene pool (i.e. the total genetic complement of the population) as a result of inbreeding. This situation could produce more rapid evolutionary changes than by natural selection alone. As the size of the population increases the chances of these non-adaptive mutations becoming established in the gene pool are reduced and selection for adaptive mutations to local conditions becomes the primary mechanism of evolutionary change. This process of rapid evolution may be used to explain the distinctive populations of animals which occur where islands near large land masses are colonized by species in which transport across the seas is a rare or accidental event. The British Isles has many such species which differ from those on the mainland of Europe and are regarded as subspecies of the continental forms. Similarly species of the Long-tailed fieldmouse *Apodemus*, the Bank vole *Clethrionomys* and the Short-tailed vole *Microtus* which occur in Britain have subspecies on the islands of St Kilda, the Hebrides and Shetland.

Animal populations can become isolated or divided as a result of many physical changes (for example, earthquakes, land subsidence, glaciation or developing river systems) which may divide the habitat of a species. This situation is believed to have occurred where the Colorado River has formed the Grand Canyon, sharply separating the Ground squirrel species *Citellus leucurus* on the north side from *C. harrisii* on the south side. The ranges of the two species do not overlap above or below the Canyon so that, as a result of different selective pressures, one or both populations have undergone sufficient change for us to regard them as separate species. The degree of geographical isolation necessary for speciation to occur depends on the active and passive dispersive ability of the animal concerned. On the South Sea Islands distinctive populations of land snails can be recognized in wooded valleys separated by dry treeless ridges. These snails have high mutation rates and poor dispersive powers: individuals rarely cross the ridges, so that each isolated gene pool undergoes mutation and selection independently. Birds have greater dispersive powers than most other animals so that the tendency for species to be split up into a series of differentiated, locally adapted populations is often counter-balanced by migration and inbreeding between such populations. This

An example of sympatric species in Britain, with four species of tits living in the same wood, able

results in the levelling out of differences between them.

On isolated islands or groups of islands, such as the Galapagos Archipelago, different populations are isolated from one another by the intervening sea. In the case of *Darwin's finches, subfamily Geospizinae, some 13 species and subspecies of finches are believed to have evolved from a single species which probably migrated about 620 miles (1,000 km) from South America. A number of populations were established among the 16 major islands. These were sufficiently isolated from one another for divergence in structure to occur as a result of genetic drift and for different selective pressures imposed by the different conditions on each island to operate. These may then be regarded as examples of allopatric species or subspecies. From time to time a flock of birds must have migrated from one island to another. Compared with their relations still living on that island they might then be regarded as sympatric species provided firstly that sufficient differences existed between the immigrants and residents for inbreeding to be rare or absent, and secondly that the populations occupied different niches. Today, some relationship can be seen between the degree of isolation of different islands or island groups within the Galapagos Archipelago and the number of

to co-exist because they occupy different niches in the habitat, but not interbreeding. From left to right, the birds are Coal tit, Blue tit, Great tit, Marsh tit.

resident species. The most isolated islands have from one to four endemic species. With decreasing isolation, however, the chances of inter-island migration rise and, as a result, representatives of changing populations may come in contact at any stage of their evolutionary divergence, and so may change from being barely distinguishable from the 'parent' species to being full subspecies. Such

islands therefore contain a greater diversity of species, subspecies and varieties than the more isolated islands. None of the islands has all 13 finches since some of the species compete with one another for food resources and therefore cannot co-exist. However, sufficient niche specialization has occurred, with associated modifications in body form and behaviour, for ten species to co-exist on

some islands. A similar situation, where sympatric species co-exist in a habitat by virtue of their different niches, occurs in Britain where Great, Blue, Coal and Marsh tits (*Parus* spp) may all be common in a single wood. This is possible because they tend to feed at different heights above the ground, at different distances from the main tree trunk and with various feeding preferences.

Example of both an allopatric and a sympatric species. On left, a population of Ground squirrels occupied both sides of the Colorado River. Being separated by the river, each population gave rise to a distinct species (centre), the White-tailed antelope ground squirrel to the north of the river, the Yuma antelope ground squirrel to the south. The two species were allopatric. Today, some of the White-tailed have crossed the river and occupy the same area (left, vertical hatching) as the Yuma but the two have different habitats and do not interbreed. In this area they are sympatric.

A number of complex isolating mechanisms have been evolved in animal populations. In the case of allopatric species, interbreeding between the two species is prevented by geographical or spatial isolation. As a result, there is no necessity or opportunity for isolating mechanisms to evolve (though these may nevertheless appear as a result of the accumulation of minor differences in genetic constitution, behaviour etc.). Therefore, if the two 'species' are brought together they may interbreed. This is the case with the Blue-winged teal *Anas discors* and the Cinnamon teal *A. cyanoptera* which produce fertile hybrids and in time form a single mixed population. The natural overlap of species, as sympatric species, can only continue if the species have evolved isolating mechanisms which prevent the gradual blurring of the species by the formation of hybrids. These isolating mechanisms can be subdivided into a number of categories. Isolation by habitat is seen in the Three-spined stickleback *Gasterosteus acul-*

eatus which has freshwater and brackish-water populations which cannot hybridize since the adults are confined to waters of different salinities during the breeding season. Seasonal isolation occurs where different species lack synchrony of their breeding cycles with regard to mating behaviour. Mechanical isolation is usually the non-correspondence between genitalia and is a frequent isolating mechanism in insects and arachnids. The prevention of fertilization is frequently maintained by a lack of attraction between eggs and sperm of different species, or a lack of penetrating power of the sperm. Other isolating mechanisms involve the non-survival of hybrids, the failure of hybrids to produce functional sex cells or, in the case of fertile and viable hybrids, a reduction in the fertility and viability of subsequent generations. Any one of these processes acting by itself could be sufficient to prevent the merging of two populations; usually, however, several are found to be acting in any given case.   J.M.A.

SYMPHYLA, little known arthropods, possibly related to primitive insects, such as *bristletails. The 100 species are white, up to $\frac{1}{3}$ in (8 mm) long, and they live in leaf litter and under stones and logs feeding on decaying plant and animal matter. Some are pests of root and other vegetable crops. The body consists of 14 segments with 12 pairs of legs, the larvae hatching with six or seven segments. The head bears long antennae. CLASS: Symphyla, PHYLUM: Arthropoda.

SYNAPSIDA, a subclass of extinct reptiles which showed many features in their skeleton resembling those found in mammals, especially in the bony arch which corresponded with the zygomatic arch or cheek bone in human beings. These reptiles appear to have given rise to the mammals and are sometimes referred to as *mammal-like reptiles. SUBCLASS: Synapsida, CLASS: Reptilia.

SYNECOLOGY, see entry on autecology and synecology.

T

TABULATE CORALS, also known as tabulates, are an extinct group of Palaeozoic corals generally included in the subclass Zoantharia (Cnidaria) but without very definite evidence. Only colonial forms are known and the colonies show considerable variation in form from creeping stem-like structures with polyps at intervals to densely packed coral-heads. The group gets its name from the conspicuous development of transverse partitions (tabulae) in the corallites. The corallite is the skeleton of an individual polyp. Vertical partitions are almost completely absent so little is known about the arrangement of mesenteries during life. Tabulates range from the Upper Cambrian to the end of the Permian, a period of roughly 275 million years which ended 225 million years ago. They were especially abundant during the Silurian and Devonian and contributed, with the *Rugose corals, to the formation of extensive coral reefs. SUBCLASS: Zoantharia, CLASS: Anthozoa, PHYLUM: Cnidaria.

TADPOLES, the larvae of frogs and toads. An aquatic larval stage is characteristic of all amphibians but in the salamanders and newts the larva is similar in appearance to the adult while in frogs and toads the tadpole looks completely different from the adult. It is more or less globular in shape, with no sharp distinction between the head and the rest of the body, and there is a long, muscular tail with a membranous crest on both its dorsal and ventral edges.

Even though the tadpole is free-living and obtains its own food it is still considered as part of the embryology of the frog or toad because until the adult form is reached all the organs of the body are not fully developed.

The development of each species of frog or toad is characteristic of that species and the time which it takes and the shape and size of the tadpole vary from species to species. There is, however, a basic pattern and this is

Tadpoles of Common frog of Europe *Rana temporaria*, with external gills, clinging to the jelly capsules from which they hatched.

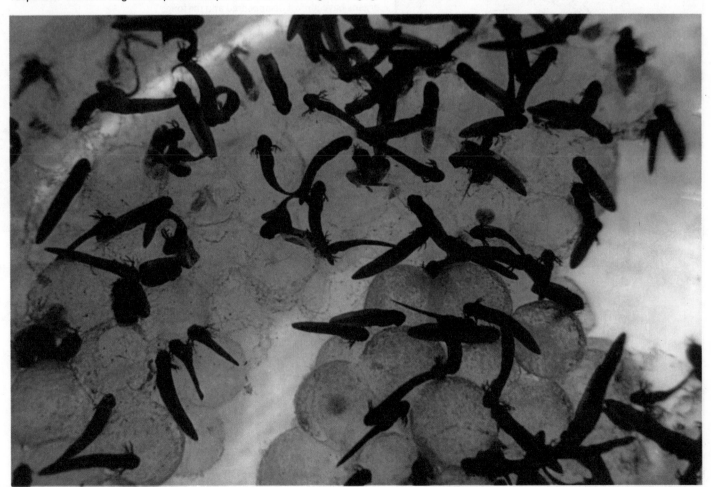

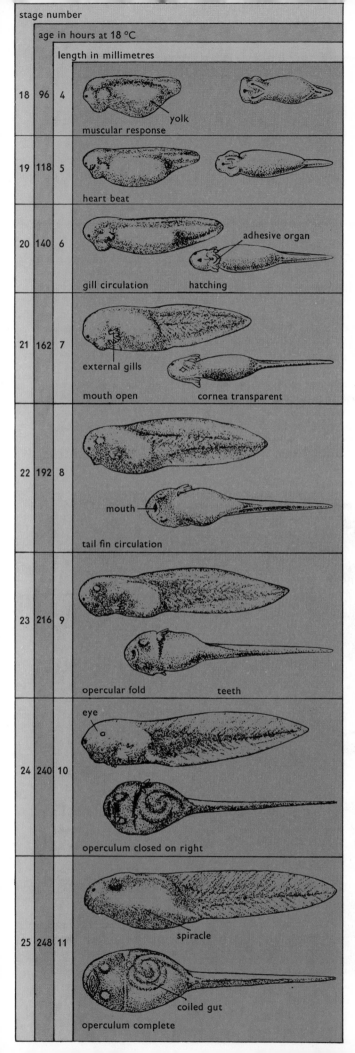

stage number	age in hours at 18 °C	length in millimetres	
18	96	4	muscular response — yolk
19	118	5	heart beat
20	140	6	gill circulation — hatching — adhesive organ
21	162	7	external gills — mouth open — cornea transparent
22	192	8	mouth — tail fin circulation
23	216	9	opercular fold — teeth
24	240	10	eye — operculum closed on right
25	248	11	spiracle — coiled gut — operculum complete

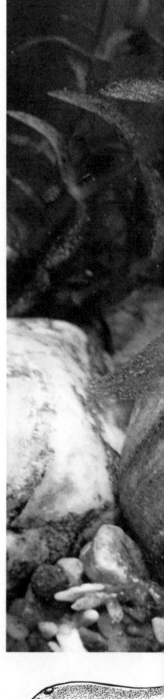

best understood by following the development of a single species, the North American Leopard frog, *Rana pipiens*. The fertilized egg divides many times and the spherical mass of cells so formed begins to differentiate into different structures. Eventually the embryo assumes a tadpole-like shape and can be seen moving inside the egg membrane. The muscular and circulation systems then develop and bulges on either side of the head show where the gill arches are forming. The external gills develop and the tadpole hatches from the egg just before these begin to function. On hatching the eyes and mouth are not fully developed and there is a U-shaped adhesive organ under the head. With this the tadpole remains attached to vegetation. The external gills function for only a short period and internal gills develop and take over from them. A fold, known as the operculum, develops on the first branchial arch just in front of the external gills and grows backwards over them until they are covered. The operculum does not close up completely and a single hole, or spiracle, remains on the left side of the body. Water is taken in through the mouth, passes over the internal gills and is expelled through the spiracle. The operculum is complete after about 12 days and by this time the mouth has developed horny jaws and several rows of horny teeth, the adhesive organs have almost disappeared and the long, coiled intestine has developed and can be seen through the skin. The tadpole is then fully developed and remains in this form until metamorphosis occurs after about three months.

When the tadpole hatches the remains of the yolk can be seen as a bulge in the belly region. This is soon used up and the tadpole then obtains its own food, which consists of small particles of vegetation, by scraping it up with the horny teeth and beak.

At metamorphosis the tadpole changes rapidly into a small frog. The hindlimbs are already visible and the forelimbs, which have been developing under the operculum, emerge—the left one through the spiracle and the right one through the skin. The internal gills cease to function and are replaced by lungs. The tadpole skin is shed, together with the horny jaws and teeth, and the mouth widens. The gut shortens since the adult is carnivorous and does not require the long gut of the herbivorous tadpole. The reproductive organs are formed and the metamorphosed frog is ready to leave the water. In the last

Stages in the development of the frog *Rana pipiens*.

Right: tadpole mouths are often correlated with the type of habitat or method of feeding. Shown here are A. *Ascaphus truei*, a mountain-brook form which clings to rocks and feeds on films of algae on the rock surface, and B. *Microhyla heymonsi*, whose umbrella mouth is used in surface film feeding.

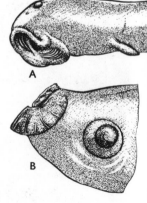

Tadpoles of *R. temporaria* at a later stage, when they have internal gills and have become carnivorous, feeding on a stickleback carcass.

stages of metamorphosis the tail slowly becomes shorter and eventually disappears, although when the young frog finally leaves the water it may still have a short tail.

The rate of development of the tadpole depends on the temperature and for this reason any reference to the age of a tadpole should include a temperature. For example, the tail bud is formed after 84 hours at 63°F (18°C) and after only 66 hours at 77°F (25°C). An indication of the point of development a tadpole has reached is also given by its length, but this will also vary slightly, depending on the available food and other factors. Although tadpoles are usually smaller than the adult frog they are sometimes larger. Tadpoles of the genus *Pseudis*

are as much as 10 in (25 cm) long while the adult is about 3 in (7·5 cm) long. See Pseudidae and Paradoxical frog.

Although the tadpole is only a stage in the development of the adult frog it is just as capable as the adult of being adapted to its environment. The round-bodied active tadpole of *R. pipiens* is the commonest type and is typically a pond-dwelling form, but the tadpoles of many species are modified for other habitats. Some tadpoles live in fast-flowing mountain streams and do not swim in the water but attach themselves to rocks. Those of the Tailed frog *Ascaphus truei* and Ghost frogs *Heleophryne* have lips forming a large cup-shaped adhesive apparatus while in others, such as *Rana cavitympanum*, the

ventral surface of the body is adapted to perform a similar function.

Many species of frogs lay their eggs in more unusual situations and often out of water altogether. *Hyla rosenbergi* lays its eggs in small pools of water retained in a mud basin constructed by the female. The tadpoles live in the basins and, because of the low oxygen content of the water, have very large external gills which float on the surface. See treefrogs.

Tadpoles of *Hoplophryne rogersi* hatch from the eggs in the stems of bamboo or between the leaves of bananas. There is very little water in these situations and the tadpoles probably remain exposed to the air for most of their development. At hatching lungs are already fully developed and external gills are never formed, while the internal ones are very reduced. The tadpole has a triangular flap of skin on either side of the body in the gill region and these are probably locomotory organs, the tadpole being able to push itself along with them.

Many species of frogs have developed similar methods of avoiding the free-swimming tadpole stage by laying the eggs out of water. The tadpoles may remain in the moist earth until they metamorphose as, for example, in *Anhydrophryne*, while in some species they are carried around by the adult. In Darwin's frog *Rhinoderma darwinii* the male carries the tadpoles in its vocal sac where they develop normally although the beaks and horny teeth do not become hardened.

In some species the complete development takes place inside the egg and it is a small frog which hatches out, although the tadpole stage is still passed through inside the egg capsule. In such situations internal gills are of little use and the tadpole is modified to obtain oxygen which diffuses in through the capsule. For example, the tadpole of the Marsupial frog *Gastrotheca marsupiata* has the external gills expanded into large bell-shaped structures while in *Platymantis* no external gills are developed and the tadpole has two large abdominal sacs well supplied with blood for respiration. Such tadpoles do not feed, of course, but depend on a large supply of yolk for the entire development.

Although in some species, for example, the Rain frogs *Breviceps*, the habit of passing the tadpole stage out of water has enabled the frog to become completely independent of water; in most cases it is probably an adaptation to avoid predators. Free-swimming tadpoles are eaten in large numbers by many fish, Water beetles and other enemies and of the large number of eggs laid by most frogs only a small proportion survives the rigours of the tadpole stage and metamorphosis. Frogs which have avoided this dangerous period usually lay fewer eggs than do those with a free-swimming tadpole stage. This is partly because such large numbers are not necessary but in any case the eggs must be larger since they have to contain enough yolk for the whole development. The development of a life-cycle which avoids the free-living tadpole stage would appear to enable such frogs to radiate into many more habitats but this is apparently not the case. The conditions under which such frogs are able to lay their eggs—in holes constructed under leaf litter, for instance—are so specialized that, in fact, the frogs are restricted as to the places in which they can breed. Only a few species have developed such methods and

Metamorphosing tadpole of *R. temporaria*, with limbs complete and just before absorption of tail.

the large majority of frogs possess free-swimming tadpoles.

Although the arrangement of horny beaks and teeth around the mouth described for the Leopard frog is the common pattern, enabling the tadpole to scrape food particles off vegetation, some frogs have a different method of obtaining food. Those of the family Microhylidae have no beaks or teeth and feed on small organisms suspended in the water, filtering them from the water as it passes through the opercular chamber. Tadpoles of *Ooeidozyga* are predaceous and have the horny beaks but lack the teeth. Some species have 'umbrella mouths' in which the lips are produced into a large funnel around the mouth. In *Microhyla heymonsi* it is used in feeding on food particles in the surface film of the water.

This brief review indicates the ways in which tadpoles are adapted to their environment, completely independently of the mode of life of the adult. Nevertheless the variations in tadpoles which lead to the evolution of such adaptations can only be transmitted from generation to generation through the adult frog. Therefore any basic differences underlying the adaptations should reveal relationships between the tadpoles which parallel those of the adults.

Variations in two characters, the spiracle and the mouth apparatus, have been used to help decide the relationships between different families of frogs. The spiracle may be on the left of the body of the tadpole, as in the Leopard frog, or it may be central or it may be paired, and the mouth may either have horny beaks and teeth or lack these structures, these different combinations giving four types of tadpoles.   M.E.D.

TADPOLE SHRIMPS, freshwater crustaceans of unusual appearance. A large rounded carapace and an elongated trunk give them their characteristic appearance and their common name. This extends from the back of the head over the front part of the trunk, but is quite free from the trunk. The head has a rounded front border, and there are two large kidney shaped eyes close together. Showing through the wall of the carapace on each side is a coiled tube, the excretory organ. On the underside of the head are two very small pairs of antennae. The mandibles are large and powerful. Behind these is a series of trunk limbs, the first of which are very elongated and act as feelers which compensate for the small size of the antennae. The trunk limbs vary in number up to 71 pairs, but the number of trunk segments is always lower, reaching a maximum of 44. This means that some trunk segments bear several pairs of limbs.

The trunk limbs beat in a rhythm in which successive limbs are slightly out of phase. Particles are swept up from the surface of

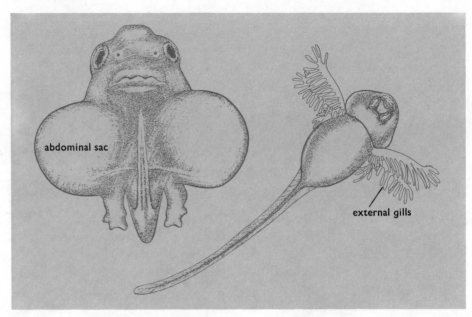

Two types of respiration in tadpoles: (left) *Platymantis hazelae*, which uses abdominal sacs, and (right) *Hyla rosenbergi*, which uses external gills.

mud, and are passed backwards along the series of limbs, all the time travelling inwards towards the midline. When the particles reach the midline they are passed forwards to the mouth by a series of projections at the bases of the limbs. As the limbs are out of phase one limb will still be moving forwards while the one in front is moving backwards. The front limb will thus collect material from the overlapping base of the limb behind and in turn pass it forwards to the next limb in front. As well as feeding on small particles Tadpole shrimps can tear pieces off larger particles using the spiny bases of some of the trunk limbs near the mouth. *Lepidurus* is known to feed on the *Fairy shrimp *Branchinecta paludosa*. It is seized by the trunk limbs and then minced by their spiny bases before being pushed into the mouth.

Tadpole shrimps are widespread throughout the world, but are irregular and erratic in their occurrence. Most species live in temporary pools. *Triops cancriformis*, the only British species, is extremely rare. The same species is often abundant in certain parts of Europe, particularly in ricefields in the South of France and in Spain, where they sometimes cause damage by uprooting rice seedlings.

The eggs are laid into brood pouches on the eleventh pair of trunk limbs. Some species lay eggs with sticky coats and after a few days in the brood pouch they are stuck onto a plant or a stone in the water. These eggs resemble those of Fairy shrimps and Clam shrimps in being capable of resisting freezing and drying. In desert regions they may have to lie dormant for several years before sufficient rain falls to form a pool for them to hatch.

The sexes may be separate, or there may be

hermaphrodites. There is variation in this from species to species, and even geographically within one species. In Western Europe most populations of *Triops cancriformis* consist of hermaphrodites, but in North Africa, in the same species, the sexes are separate.

The eggs give rise to nauplius larvae, which swim by means of their antennae, not by trunk limbs, the adult method. *Lepidurus arcticus* is an exceptional species which hatches at a more advanced stage of development. This lives in arctic pools and lakes which are unfrozen for only a few months in the year, so it is essential that individuals hatching in the early summer become mature and lay eggs before the water freezes again. Its eggs are larger than those of other Tadpole shrimps and the larvae are larger and better developed than the nauplius larvae of other species. They have, for instance, a well developed carapace and several trunk limbs, although they still swim by means of their antennae.

Tadpole shrimps are living fossils. One of the nine present-day species *Triops cancriformis*, is known as a fossil from the Triassic period, over 150 million years ago. ORDER: Notostraca, SUBCLASS: Branchiopoda, CLASS: Crustacea, PHYLUM: Arthropoda.
                                                                   Ja.G.

TAHR, a close relative of the goat. Males have a characteristic odour, a little different from that of the 'billy-goat'. There is no beard, and the horns are short, highly compressed bilaterally and keeled in front; they are simply backcurved. The Himalayan tahr *Hemitragus jemlahicus* is 36–40 in (90–100 cm) high. Big males weigh 200 lb (90 kg), but females may weigh only 80 lb (35 kg).

The taipan of Australasia, reputed to be the most dangerous of all snakes.

It has a heavy body, narrow ears and coarse shaggy hair which forms a mane on the neck and shoulders, reaching to the knees. It is brown with a dorsal stripe. It is found along the Himalayas from Kashmir to Sikkim, on precipitous cliffs, in scrub and forest, from 10–12,000 ft (3,050–3,660 m).

The Nilgiri tahr *H. hylocrius* is slightly bigger, 39–42 in (100–110 cm), with a short yellow-brown coat, old males becoming deep brown with a distinct light 'saddle-patch' on the back. Females have only one pair of teats; other species have two. It is found from the Nilgiris to the Anaimalais, south along the western Ghats at 4–6,000 ft (1,220–1,830 m), on scarps and crags above the forest.

The Arabian tahr *H. jayakari* is small, only 24–26 in (60–65 cm) high, slenderly built, sandy with a dorsal crest but, like the Nilgiri tahr, no mane. It has long shaggy hair, however. It is restricted to the mountains of Oman.

The Himalayan tahr has been introduced to New Zealand and South Africa. In South Africa, a pair were enclosed, some 30 years ago, in a paddock on Groote Schuur estate on Table Mountain; they leaped over the 5 ft fence and escaped. Some 50 now live there. In New Zealand, an original 11 have bred and now populate much of the southern Alps.

Male tahr live solitary lives most of the year. Unlike females, they never, at least in the Himalayan species, graze in open clearings, but emerge from the oak and cane forests only in the evenings. They migrate up and down the slopes according to season and snowfall. The rut takes place in the winter and rams are often killed by falling during the fierce fights. Little else is known about the breeding of these animals. FAMILY: Bovidae, ORDER: Artiodactyla, CLASS: Mammalia. C.P.G.

TAILOR-BIRDS, two genera of warblers. The nine species of *Orthotomus* are found in southern Asia, from India to the Philippines. They are common garden birds and are named after their method of nest-building, in which leaves are stitched together with fibres to form a pouch. The Australian tailor-bird, or Golden-headed fantail-warbler *Cisticola exilis*, makes a similar nest. FAMILY: Sylviidae, ORDER: Passeriformes, CLASS: Aves.

TAIPAN *Oxyuranus scutellatus*, a slender *elapid snake and the largest and deadliest of Australasian snakes, growing to a little over 11 ft (3·4 m) in length. It has a large head distinct from its neck, a relatively slim fore-body and tapered tail. Its fangs are large and its venom one of the most potent neurotoxins known; death is usually caused by paralysis of the nerve centres controlling the lungs and heart. It is reputed to be the world's deadliest snake. Australian taipans are rich brown above and cream below, while those from New Guinea are usually blackish with a rusty-red stripe along the middle of the back.

The taipan is found throughout many parts of northern and north-eastern Australia, ranging from coastal rain-forests to the drier inland regions. In New Guinea it is found largely in the savannah woodlands along the southern coasts. About 16 eggs are laid in a clutch. The taipan is a timid, retiring snake which may become very aggressive when provoked. It may be seen in weather conditions that are too hot for other snakes, and although generally diurnal, it may move about at night if the weather has been excessively hot. It feeds upon small mammals and reptiles.

Specific and polyvalent antivenenes have been developed for the taipan, without which the chances of recovering from a bite are slender. The name taipan is a Cape York aboriginal name for this snake. FAMILY: Elapidae, ORDER: Squamata, CLASS: Reptilia. H.G.C.

TAKAHE *Notornis mantelli*, a large, flightless bird of New Zealand. Sub-fossil remains show that it was recently widely distributed, but in the 19th century European settlers found only five specimens. It was thought to be extinct until its dramatic rediscovery in a remote, high, tussock-grassland valley in 1948.

Extensive study since then has shown it to be in danger of extinction with only 300 birds left in an area of 200 sq miles (533 sq km). Numbers seem to have been shrinking before the arrival of Europeans, suggesting that the Polynesians were probably responsible for the decline. The takahe does not breed successfully in captivity but attempts are being made to establish it in other parts of New Zealand. FAMILY: Rallidae, ORDER: Gruiformes, CLASS: Aves.

TAKIN *Budorcas taxicolor*, an ungainly-looking goat-antelope related to the musk-ox. 42 in (110 cm) high, weighing 500–600 lb (230–275 kg), takin have a convex face, heavy muzzle, thick neck, short thick legs, humped shoulders and an arched back. The colour is golden to dark brown or black on the flanks and haunches (according to race); the withers are always lighter toned. Calves are black. The horns, found in both sexes, are thick and triangular in section. They are at first upright, then turn out, then up at the tips. Takin are found along the flanks of the mountains from Bhutan through Szechwan to Shensi. They inhabit steep, thickly wooded slopes, most characteristically the dense bamboo and rhododendron jungle at 7–10,000 ft (2,135–3,050 m), but in the Mishmi hills of northern Assam they go as low as 3–4,000 ft (9–1,200 m). They keep in the forest by day, feeding and drinking at open springs, even at hot springs, in the morning and evening. In summer, takin sometimes enter the stunted bush zone of the Szechwan plateau and, at this time, they may form herds of up to 300. In autumn and winter these break up into smaller parties, the bulls each joining with one or more cows. The small herds make regular paths through the vegetation. When disturbed, they crash off with a warning cough.

During the rut, which in Szechwan takes place in July to August, the males, which are always aggressive, are extremely dangerous, and fight fiercely. Gestation lasts about 200 days and calves are born in early April. The cow enters the forest to give birth. FAMILY: Bovidae, ORDER: Artiodactyla, CLASS: Mammalia.

TAMANDUA *Tamandua tetradactyla,* an anteater intermediate in size between the Giant and the tiny Silky species and, like them, is completely toothless and belongs to the mammalian order Edentata along with the sloths and armadillos. The tamandua is also called the Prehensile-tailed anteater or the Collared anteater (from its most typical colour pattern).

Tamanduas have short coarse hair on the body and on top of the tail near its base, but most of the grasping tail is naked and blotched with irregular markings. Tamanduas vary greatly in colouration, but typically they have a black band encircling the middle of the body and this joins, on the back, a black ring or 'collar' around the neck. Head and legs are tan or cream-coloured so the animals look as if they are wearing a dark vest or waistcoat. The ears are rounded but more conspicuous and proportionately larger than those of the Giant anteater. Fox-sized, the tamandua has a head and body length of 21–22·5 in (54–58 cm) with a 21 in (54 cm) tail. Tamanduas have the characteristic anteater spout-like snout (ideal for poking into rotting logs and termite nests) and long extensile tongue, no bigger in diameter than a lead pencil. The nostrils and the tiny mouth are at the tip of the snout. The nails of the hands are long and sharp, particularly those of the middle fingers, and tamanduas have great strength in their arms and tearing power in their claws.

The tamandua ranges from southern Mexico to Argentina and is found in tropical forests and occasionally savannahs. Little is known of its reproductive biology except that the single young apparently is carried on the mother's back from birth.

Whereas the Giant anteater is almost entirely terrestrial and the Silky predominately arboreal, the tamandua is equally at home in the trees and on the ground, walking on the edges of its palms with claws turned in, but nevertheless it seems to spend most of its time in trees, being an excellent climber, and its prehensile tail suggests a long history of arboreal living. Tamanduas are active mainly at night but often stir in daytime, emerging from their tree hollows in early morning and late afternoon to forage for a variety of ants, tree- and ground-nesting termites, and bees. The insects adhere to the tamandua's tongue made sticky by a coating of viscous saliva when the animal is feeding. Like its larger cousin the Giant anteater, the tamandua consumes great quantities of insects. The stomach of one individual examined contained 1 lb (0·45 kg) of ants. In the tamandua part of the stomach is a muscular gizzard, presumably to compensate for the lack of teeth and to permit digestion of hard-shelled ants. The ants are ground in much the same way as grain is ground by the gizzards of gallinaceous birds.

Tamanduas defend themselves in typical anteater fashion by rearing up on their haunches and slashing out with the claws. In

The takin of the wooded mountains of southern Asia, one of the goat-antelopes.

trees, the hindlegs and tail act both as supports and anchor for the animal, leaving the arms free for action. If attacked on the ground, tamanduas try to protect their backs by rearing against a tree, rock or other barrier. They are seemingly unable to gallop away when alarmed as will the Giant anteater.

Although relatively common in the wild, tamanduas are one of the most difficult mammals to keep in captivity despite the fact that their natural diet seems to differ little from that of the more hardy Giant anteater. They are reported to be gentler and more tractable than the Giants, but they seldom survive more than a few months after capture, and the record life span (based on a single individual) is just under five years. FAMILY: Myrmecophagidae, ORDER: Edentata, CLASS: Mammalia. M.M.W.

TAMARAO *Bubalus (Bubalus) mindorensis,* a small species of buffalo from the island of Mindoro in the Philippines, closely related to the Water buffalo, and by some authorities, such as H. Bohlken, classed as a subspecies of it. It differs considerably from the Water buffalo in its small size, being only 40 in (1 m) high, much stouter and more robust build, its short and very thick horns, and its colour, which is jet black with white bands above the hoofs only instead of white shanks. Tamarao weigh 600–700 lb (270–320 kg) and the horns are only 14–20 in (35·5–51 cm) long and slightly incurved. In breeding it is very similar to other bovids.

In historic times the tamarao occurred on Luzon as well as Mindoro. Now, however, its existence is threatened even on its remaining island. Up to five years ago, small groups or individuals could be seen grazing in the open, but today they are largely nocturnal having been shot by farmers with whose stock they compete, for grazing. Groups up to 11 have been seen, but most are solitary. Its numbers and distribution have been reduced by cultivation and lumbering, and now it is most common on Mt Iglit, seeming to have left the lowlands altogether. In 1964, L. M. Talbot estimated that about 200–250 were still in existence, but by 1965 the IUCN had revised this estimate to a mere 100 or so. The tamarao is one of the most gravely endangered living mammals.

The name is sometimes spelt 'tamarau' or 'tamaraw'. FAMILY: Bovidae, ORDER: Artiodactyla, CLASS: Mammalia.

TAMARIN *Saguinus,* small species of *marmoset found in South and Central America.

TAMING, the elimination in animals of tendencies to flee in the presence of man. Some wild animals may already be unafraid of man, as are the birds and sealions of the Galapagos Islands, but most require taming if a close relationship with man is to be established; even domesticated animals require taming if such an association has not been formed early in their lives.

Under natural conditions animals are shy and wary and although there is no evidence that they inherit a specific fear of man there is a general tendency of distrust towards ground-living predators. When a predator or man approaches within a certain distance the animal will attempt to flee; the distance at which the animal will take flight varies according to its species, age and previous experience. Parental training may also reinforce the shyness. The flight distance, however, may be reduced and the escape reaction modified if the animal becomes habituated to the presence of man as a harmless nonpredator. Young animals in particular show less fear and are more ready to establish social contacts; some of the more precocious may even become imprinted on man and start following him around, for example, young seals.

When the flight tendency has been sufficiently reduced for capture to be possible the animal loses its freedom and undergoes a transitional stage of adaptation to a new environment. It becomes completely dependent on man for its food, bedding, shelter and the provision of a safe enclosure as its territory. A social relationship is established and the animal becomes emotionally stable in the presence of man at close quarters. Yet regressions can occur, and frights or sudden movements may reverse the process or even precipitate attack. Some animals on the other hand become so attached to man himself that they become antisocial towards their own species, which they treat as aliens.

Taming was the first stage in the process of domestication of dogs, goats, sheep, cattle, pigs, horses and the other animals of economic importance to man. Taming is also the first essential in the care and management of wild animals kept for exhibition in zoos. Nevertheless, even species which have been domesticated for thousands of years will quickly revert to feral types if animal/man contact is lost, and the flight distance will dramatically increase. Domestication has resulted in animals being selected for tameness, adaptability and desirable characteristics of economic importance, so feral animals seldom revert completely to the behaviour-pattern of their wild ancestors.

Taming any animal involves infinite patience and a deep understanding of its requirements. A quiet approach, expert handling and confidence are probably the essential human attributes. Animals which have already been trained are used to motivate others by example in the right direction. Rewards for satisfactory performances are appreciated and in certain cases may be demanded. The tame animal, however, particularly if it is of a non-domesticated species, can be dangerous, for it has lost its sense of fear and if thwarted in a particular desire it can become quite suddenly violent and aggressive. W.N.S.

TANAGERS, small colourful birds of the family of Thraupidae. There are about 200 species all confined to the New World, ranging from southern North America, through Central America and the West Indies to the tropical parts of South America. The largest number of species lives in the tropical areas.

Tanagers vary in size from that of a tit to that of a finch. Many of them, especially those living in the tropics, are brilliantly coloured. Among these are the members of the genera *Euphonia* (20 species) and *Tangara* (43 species). The euphonias are the smallest and in most of them the males have glossy blue upperparts and yellow or orange underparts. The females are quite different, having a dull green plumage which makes them difficult to distinguish in the field. They live in trees and shrubbery at forest edges and feed mainly on the berries of mistletoes. Euphonias make dome-shaped nests with a side entrance, sometimes between the leaves of tree orchids. The nests are built by both sexes and the female lays three to four eggs which is more than most other tanagers.

Even more colourful are some members of the genus *Tangara* of which the Paradise tanager *Tangara chilensis* is perhaps the finest. It is velvety black on its upperparts, while the crown and the sides of the face are green. The lower back is scarlet, the rump yellow and the underparts are mostly turquoise blue with the lower underparts black. As in most tangaras the sexes are alike and somewhat larger than the euphonias. They live in groups in tree-tops at forest edges and feed on fruit. The tangaras make open cup nests, which are built by both sexes, and lay only two eggs.

One of the best known tanagers is the Blue-grey tanager *Thraupis episcopus* which has a large distribution, occurring from southern Mexico south through Central America to Bolivia. It is blue-grey with sky blue wings, the sexes being alike. It is quite a common garden bird in some parts of its range. The Blue-grey tanager makes an open cup nest of dead grasses and leaves, lined with a thick layer of dead grasses. It is built by both sexes. It lays one or two eggs which are incubated by the female only, the nestlings, however, are fed by both parents. It lives on fruit but also takes insects, for example flying termites which are captured in flight.

Of about the same size are the members of the genus *Tachyphonus* with nine species. The males of this genus are largely black with yellow or red markings, but the females are totally different. They live in groups in the tree-tops and are often associated with other species of the family. One of them, the Red-shouldered tanager *Tachyphonus phoenicius,* inhabits savannahs covered with scattered bushes and makes an open cup nest on the ground. This is an exception among the tanagers.

On the whole tanagers are poor songsters, yet some of them, especially the euphonias, are popular cage birds which thrive in captivity. FAMILY: Thraupidae, ORDER: Passeriformes, CLASS: Aves.   F.H.

TAPACULOS, a family of about 26 species of small to medium-sized perching birds found in South and Central America. They vary from about 4–10 in (10–25 cm) long and have soft, fluffy plumage in which grey, brown or black usually predominates. They are dumpy birds that often hold the tail cocked over the back. Their legs are strong correlated with a terrestrial habit and the bill is straight, thin in the small species and

stouter in the large ones. The wings are short and rounded, and the tail varies from a short tuft to a long flag of stiff feathers.

Tapaculos live in thick cover, whether in dark woodland thickets or dry thorn scrub on the pampas. They creep or run about among the thick vegetation only rarely taking to the wing. In most of the species the male and female share the same dull colouring, but in a few, such as the Slaty bristle-front *Merulaxis ater,* the male is more brightly coloured than the female. Little is known about their feeding habits, but both insects and seeds have been found in the stomachs of several species. They feed by picking food up from the surface of the ground or off vegetation and by scratching in the litter of dead leaves, some species having very stout feet and claws as adaptations to scratching.

Although tapaculos are difficult birds to see because of their skulking habits and the dense cover in which they live, many species make their presence obvious by having very loud songs and calls. Both sexes of some species are known to sing, the songs usually consisting of a monotonous series of whistling notes. The well-known huet-huet *Pteroptochos tarnii* gives a repetitive series of notes sounding like 'wed wed wed', hence the name. The Crested or Grey gallito *Rhinocrypta lanceolata* gives chirping and tweeting calls and others, such as the tapaculos of the genus *Scytalopus,* have repetitive scratching notes that either gain or lose speed as they are given in series. Many of the calls and songs have a ventriloquial effect, making the singer hard to locate.

Most tapaculos nest in burrows in the ground; sometimes they dig a hole for themselves, sometimes they use an abandoned mammal burrow. A few species nest in hollow trees and a few others, such as the Ochre-flanked tapaculo *Eugralla paradoxa,* build ball-shaped domed nests in thickets, or on the ground as in the White-breasted babbler or White-breasted tapaculo *Scytalopus indigoticus.* Both the hole-nesters and those that nest in the open build substantial nests of grass and twigs that are lined with feathers, hair or finer vegetation. Two to four rather large white eggs are laid, these often being dirtied by the birds' feet so as to appear spotted. Incubation periods and the parts played by the sexes in incubation have not been described for any of the species. The young hatch covered with dark-coloured down and remain in the nest for some time before fledging, though no precise fledging periods are known. Most other aspects of the behaviour of these secretive birds await discovery. FAMILY: Rhinocryptidae, ORDER: Passeriformes, CLASS: Aves.   D.H.

Emerald spotted tanager *Tanager guttata.*

TAPEWORMS, internal parasites, so named because they are long and flat. The whitish body (called the strobila) is marked off into many segments, or proglottids each containing a complete set of male and female reproductive organs. The proglottids are connected by muscles, two lateral nerve cords and the two pairs of excretory ducts connecting the *flame cells. The proglottids are budded off continually from a region just behind the minute scolex, or head region, by which the long tapeworm is attached to the intestinal mucosa of the vertebrate host. At first the proglottids are very small and the reproductive organs embryonic, but farther down the strobila the proglottids become progressively more mature. In each proglottid the male organ matures first, so ensuring cross fertilization, the female system too becomes mature until in the terminal proglottids the branching uterus is packed with fertilized, shelled eggs and the gonads and eggshell forming glands have degenerated.

The Broad tapeworm of man *Diphyllobothrium latum*, is really a fish tapeworm that has become accustomed to living in man, the proglottids are added constantly throughout life but are not shed, ripe eggs simply being emitted from the uterus, so this tapeworm may have 3,000 to 4,000 proglottids and reach 10–30 ft (3–9 m) in length when mature. In most tapeworms living in terrestrial vertebrates, including man, however, the proglottids containing eggs are shed from the end of the worm and passed out in the faeces, so the strobila remains relatively constant in size once it has reached its maximum length. Even so, they can be very large; the Beef tapeworm *Taenia saginata* which man acquires by eating measly beef

attains a length of 15–20 ft (4½–6 m) and specimens of up to 50 ft (15 m) have been recorded although the scolex is only 1·5–2 mm diameter. Individual proglottids can be quite active after being detached and may wriggle around for some time.

Attachment. This enormous length of worm is attached to the gut lining by a tiny scolex. The relatively primitive tapeworms of bony fishes have a scolex armed only with two slit-like shallow suckers. Those in sharks and rays have a scolex that looks like a daffodil with four intricately sculptured, petalloid suckers borne on stalks surrounding a median, muscular sucker. Other tapeworms occurring specifically in sharks and rays have a scolex bearing four long spine-covered tentacles which can be retracted into the main body of the scolex. Tapeworms from man, his livestock and pets, in fact all terrestrial vertebrates, have a scolex armed with four suckers with a rostrum or beak in front typically bearing one or more circlets of hooks. Tapeworms are extremely specific to their vertebrate definitive hosts and have evolved in concert with them over a very long period so that related groups of vertebrates are parasitized by related groups of tapeworms.

Feeding. Tapeworms are so specialized to their way of life that they have lost their gut and absorb predigested soluble food from the host's intestine through their skin. Tapeworms seem to be much more agile than was once supposed. They can find their way to the most favourable spots where the food supply is richest and where they can attach themselves most securely. If tapeworms are surgically transplanted to a less favourable site in a different part of the gut, they will

migrate back to the preferred site. They have even been said to be able to migrate forwards to the small intestine of laboratory animals when introduced via the rectum.

It was often wondered in the past how tapeworms were able to live in the small intestine of their hosts without themselves being digested. It seems that, like the lining of the host's intestine, they are covered by a 'surface coat' of fibrous mucoprotein which is very resistant to digestion. There seem to be specific sites on this outer membrane where carrier molecules pick up particular amino acids or sugars before these are taken into the worm. There is no body cavity in tapeworms but the body is filled with parenchyma or packing tissue and this stores a great deal of carbohydrate in the form of glycogen.

Reproductive system. Cestodes have quite complicated life-cycles which may involve two intermediate hosts as well as a definitive host, so to compensate for the hazards involved in the life history a vast number of eggs is produced. In some tapeworms each proglottid contains not one but two complete sets of reproductive organs. The male system consists of a set of diffusely arranged testes which empty into a vas deferens, the end of which is developed into an evaginable muscular intromittent organ known as a cirrus which is armed with many small spines. The female system is composed, in addition to the ovary or ovaries, of a vagina to receive sperms, a seminal receptacle for sperm storage and an ootype where the egg shell is formed after fertilization, this connecting with the vitelline glands which provide raw materials for the egg shell and also food reserves. From the ootype the shelled eggs pass into the capacious uterus which

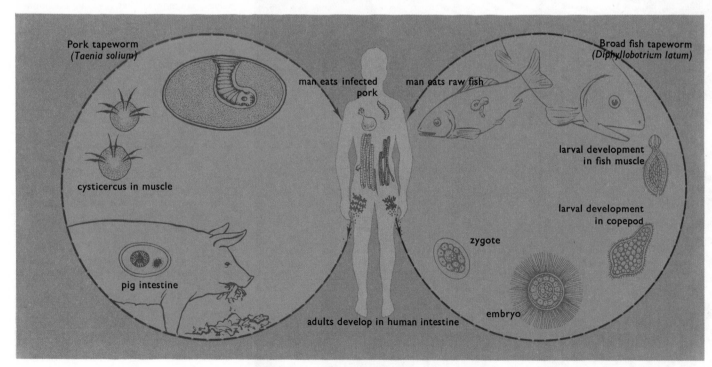

Pork tapeworm (*Taenia solium*)

man eats infected pork

man eats raw fish

Broad fish tapeworm (*Diphyllobotrium latum*)

cysticercus in muscle

larval development in fish muscle

larval development in copepod

zygote

pig intestine

adults develop in human intestine

embryo

develops side branches and in mature proglottids packs out the whole proglottis. In
most tapeworms the cirrus and vagina open
into a cup-shaped genital atrium. This is
situated on the lateral margin of the worm
and its position may alternate from side to
side in alternate proglottids or change in
various regular ways in different forms.

Life-cycles. There are two main kinds of
life-cycle in cestodes, a more primitive
aquatic life-cycle and a highly evolved terrestrial life-cycle.

The aquatic cycle involves a free swimming arthropod, usually a crustacean, an
amphipod or a copepod, as first intermediate
host, followed by a second vertebrate intermediate host which is usually a fish or
amphibian and then typically culminates in a
fish or amphibian final host. Some of these
fish tapeworms, like *Ligula* and *Schisto-
cephalus* which infect birds and *Diphyllobothrium* the Broad tapeworm of man,
occur in warm-blooded final hosts because
these hosts are fish-eaters and have acquired
the infection by habitually eating infected
fish. The life-cycle of *Diphyllobothrium latum*
will serve as an example.

The egg hatches to release a ciliated,
free-swimming coracidium larva which has
six posterior larval hooks. This is swallowed
by a copepod, loses its ciliated covering and
bores through the arthropod's gut into the
body cavity. Here it transforms into a
procercoid which is an elongate larva with a
pinched-off tail region, the cercomere, bearing the larval hooks. When the infected
copepod is eaten by a fish the procercoid
escapes, again bores through the gut wall and
develops in the muscles of the fish into a
plerocercoid larva which lacks the cercomere.
The plerocercoids of *D. latum* occur in
carnivorous fishes such as pike, trout and
perch and may reach a size of several
centimetres in the muscles of these hosts.
When a small fish harbouring a plerocercoid
larva of *D. latum* is eaten by a larger fish host
the larva is able to penetrate the gut of the
host and pass into the body cavity and
muscles of this host; this may occur several
times until the plerocercoid is consumed by a
suitable warm-blooded animal in which the
worm can develop to the adult state in the gut.
Infection of man, dogs and cats occurs when
the undercooked raw flesh or roe of infected
fishes is consumed. The worm grows very
rapidly in the intestine of these final hosts and
may have reached a length of 3 ft (1 m) in
three weeks and have started to lay eggs by
this time. Symptoms of the infection in man
are loss of weight and abdominal pain. This
tapeworm also has an unusually high require-

Left: life-cycle in two kinds of tapeworm.

Right: one of the smallest tapeworms, *Echinococcus*, lives in the intestine of dogs, foxes and
rats.

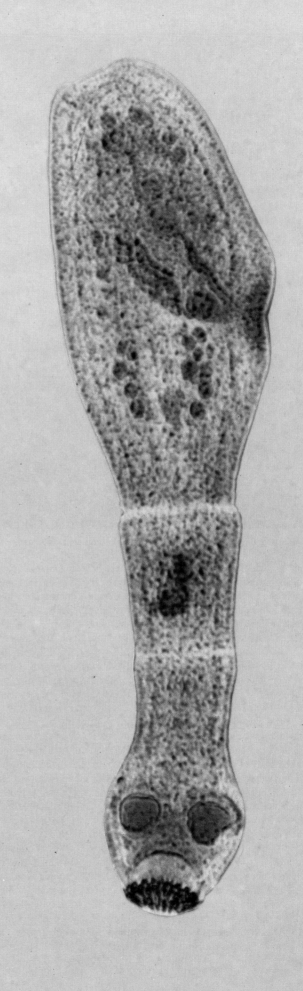

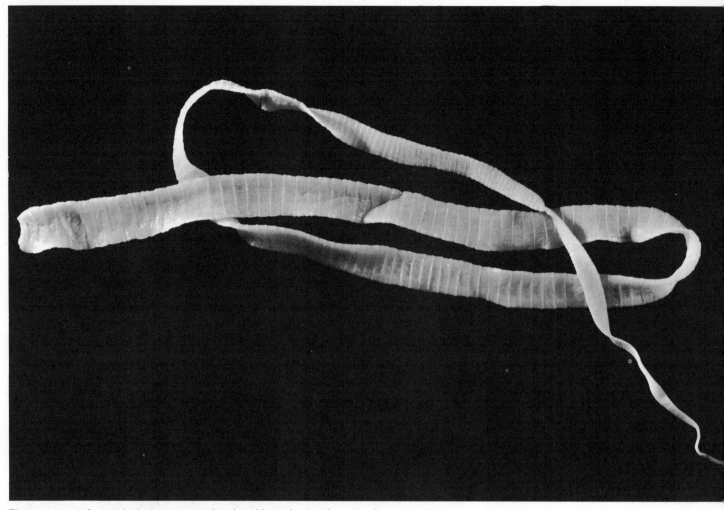

The tapeworm infesting the human intestine has the rabbit and pig as alternative hosts.

ment for vitamin B_{12} which it absorbs in great quantities from the intestine. As this vitamin is necessary for blood formation its depletion causes severe pernicious anaemia in man.

A truly terrestrial life-cycle is one in which there is no ciliated coracidium larva and in which a six-hooked oncosphere larva is ingested whilst still within the egg by a terrestrial intermediate host before infecting a terrestrial final host. Primitive terrestrial life-cycles of tapeworms involve a terrestrial arthropod, such as a Wood louse, myriapod or insect. This swallows the infective eggs and the oncosphere larva hatches within the gut, bores through the wall of the intestine and develops into a cysticercoid larva in the body cavity. The cysticercoid larva is rather like a plerocercoid but has a fully formed scolex which is retracted into the front end of the larva. The infective arthropod host then has to be eaten by the final host. This kind of life-cycle occurs in *Hymenolepis diminuta* which occasionally infects man, but is mainly a parasite of rats and mice. Grain beetles and other insect pests of stored products become infected by eating mouse or rat droppings and man then eats the infected insects present in dried fruits or cereals. In general, however,

there has been a tendency for the life-cycle in terrestrial forms to be compressed, so that an arthropod intermediate host is eliminated in favour of a vertebrate intermediate host and even to remove the necessity for an intermediate host altogether, thus making the life-cycle very efficient. *Hymenolepis nana*, the Dwarf tapeworm of man, can complete its whole life-cycle in man and is quite exceptional amongst tapeworms in this respect. This worm measures only $\frac{1}{3}$–4 in (7–100 m) in length, but often occurs in very large numbers. As is the case with many parasites, the length of the Dwarf tapeworm is inversely proportional to the number of worms present, and this could be a safety mechanism so that the host is not too seriously affected by large infections whilst at the same time competition between the worms for nutrients may be reduced so that the maximum number is supported. When eggs of *H. nana* are swallowed by man the oncosphere larvae hatch in the intestine and burrow into the villi of the intestine wall where they develop into cysticercoids in about four days. When these become mature they migrate back into the lumen of the intestine and attach to the lining using the scolex, before growing to egg

producing adults. The Dwarf tapeworm still retains the more primitive life-cycle as an alternative, however, and in this case development involves a flea or a Grain beetle and a rat or a mouse.

The large tapeworms of man include the Pork tapeworm *Taenia solium* and the Beef tapeworm *T. saginata*. As their names suggest, these use pigs and cattle respectively as their sole intermediate hosts and man acquires the infection by eating measly pork or beef. The proglottids expelled in the stools are extremely active, unlike those of the Pork tapeworm, and may even themselves creep out of the anus. In conditions where sewage disposal is primitive, eggs contaminate pasture grazed by cattle so that these become infected. Oncospheres are then liberated from the egg, penetrate the gut wall and make their way via the lymph ducts or blood vessels to the muscles, mainly the jaw muscles and heart. Here the oncosphere larva loses its six larval hooks and develops into a bladder-worm or cysticercus (plural cysticerci), in which the scolex is not merely retracted but actually invaginated into the body, which is hollow, bladder-like and filled with fluid. The cysticerci of the Beef tapeworm may measure up to $\frac{2}{5}$ in (1 cm) across. When man eats undercooked measly beef these cysticerci escape, the scolex evaginates and the worms attach to the gut wall and become adult. These tapeworm infections of domestic animals long associated with man probably explain why pork is forbidden to Moslems and Jews and beef is not eaten by Hindus. The Pork tapeworm is particularly dangerous because if the eggs of this worm are accidentally ingested by man they can develop into bladderworms in what would normally be the definitive host. If these reach the brain they may produce epileptic fits and paralysis.

Larval multiplication. Some tapeworms reproduce asexually by budding while in the intermediate host, thus increasing the chances that infection of a definitive host will occur. This larval multiplication (or polyembryony) is most highly developed in a small tapeworm, only three proglottids long, called *Echinococcus* which lives as an adult in the intestine of dogs, foxes, wolves, rats and cats. The usual intermediate hosts of *Echinococcus granulosus* are sheep and cattle, and in them a kind of 'bladderworm' develops which produces internally many daughter or brood cysts containing secondary scolices. This mother cyst is termed a hydatid cyst because it is filled with fluid. It can become very large and may reach the size of an orange and produce millions of scolices. After 10–20 years the hydatid cysts may reach an enormous size and can contain over three gallons of liquid. Man can inadvertently serve

as an intermediate host for *Echinococcus* and hydatid cysts develop as a result of infection with eggs originally liberated in dog faeces but which may be picked up from the fur or tongue of the dog after this has licked itself. Hydatid disease of man is complicated by the fact that, should the cyst containing brood capsules be ruptured, these can take root and grow in other tissues of the body. In view of the fact that the life-cycle of *Echinococcus* relies on contact between domestic ruminants and, for instance, dogs, it is hardly surprising that human hydatidosis is prevalent in sheep- and cattle-raising areas such as parts of Africa, New Zealand and Australia.

The evolutionary relationships of tapeworms. Not all cestodes are tapeworms. Some cestodes occurring usually in fish are not segmented although the gonads may be repeated down the body, as in *Caryophylleus* which occurs in the gut of freshwater rutilid fishes. These unstrobilated cestodes are thought to be neotenous plerocercoid larvae and therefore to have been secondarily derived from a segmented ancestral tapeworm.

The cestodes must have arisen from an unsegmented ancestor and it has been suggested that the reason that segmentation was developed was to replicate the number of ootypes where the egg shell and yolk are moulded around the fertilized egg, since this would be a bottleneck in the egg production line. There is some evidence that monogenean ectoparasites of fishes and the cestodes,

which are both highly specific to their final vertebrate hosts and both have larvae bearing posterior hooks, might have arisen from a common ancestral platyhelminth. As the tapeworm ancestors became highly successful endoparasites and developed efficient ways of feeding across the body wall they would have been able to dispense with a gut so that in the absence of a mouth an anterior attachment organ, the scolex, could be developed. The nutrient rich environment the worms now found themselves in would provide for the production of a large number of eggs, which would reduce the hazards of their spanning several intermediate hosts in the life-cycle and at the same time provide for the rapid asexual proliferation of proglottids in the neck region when segmentation had been evolved. The tapeworms are amongst the most highly committed and beautifully adapted of animal parasites. CLASS: Cestoda, PHYLUM: Platyhelminthes.   K.M.L.

TAPIR, a large brown or black and white ungulate with many similarities to the rhinoceros. It belongs to the order Perissodactyla and is probably the most unspecialized type of that order. Tapirs form the family, Tapiridae, which belongs with the Rhinocerotidae (rhinos) in the suborder Tapiromorpha.

They are plump, thick-skinned creatures, the males weighing about 400–800 lb (180–360 kg) and the females 200–400 lb (90–180 kg). The forefeet bear four toes; the

Brazilian tapir on the bank of the Amazon.

hindfeet, three, but the outer toes of the forefeet are small and on hard ground may not leave an imprint, so that tapir tracks are sometimes mistaken for those of small rhinos. The dental formula of the tapir is $\frac{3143}{3143}=44$, but, as in the rhinoceros, $P\frac{1}{1}$ may be unrepresented in the permanent dentition. The lower canine is well-developed but the upper is smaller than I^3. The cheekteeth are low-crowned, with no cement as tapirs are browsers. The chief external differences with rhinos are the absence of horns, the elongation of the snout into a short proboscis with terminal nostrils, the long neck, the absence of skin folds, and the presence of at least a sparse covering of hair. The skull is distinctly different, with a high narrow crown and short, high-placed nasals. In spite of the general similarity, tapirs and rhinos have been distinct since the Lower Oligocene, when clear fossils of both families—often considered indistinguishable from living genera—are found. Tapirs appeared first in Europe, later spreading to North America. Living tapirs have an oddly discontinuous distribution in Southeast Asia and in Central and South America. Because of the conservatism of tapirs and their comparative lack of change throughout their history, this distribution can hardly be used as evidence that the Bering Strait was tropical in the Pleistocene, as has sometimes been claimed.

The four living species, all placed in the single genus *Tapirus,* are not very closely related but the Malay tapir is the most distinct and can be placed in the subgenus *Acrocodia.* The three New World species all belong to the nominate subgenus and, according to Hershkovitz, who places them unnecessarily in three different subgenera, they each represent a separate invasion into South America.

The Malay tapir *Tapirus indicus* is the largest species, weighing as much as 800 lb (360 kg). It is black, with a white body and haunches. The white begins behind the forelegs and extends over the rest of the body except for the hindlegs and tail. There is no mane on the neck, the proboscis is longer than in other species and the build is heavier and stouter. Malay tapirs live in lowland, especially swamp forest, in Sumatra, Malaya, Tenasserim, southern Thailand, and formerly also in Laos, where they have been recorded at Bassac, and in northern Thailand, where they were reported at Xieng May on the Shan States frontier. In prehistoric times the tapir occurred also in Borneo and in the Pleistocene it was found in Java and China.

The Malay tapir is an inoffensive creature that is rarely seen. It lives a solitary wanderer's life, following permanent and well-used trails through the forest to water, like a rhinoceros. Although it seems to be fairly common at present, the deforestation of

its habitat is bound eventually to threaten its existence. So shy and inconspicuous is it that it will be gone before anyone is aware of it.

A Malay tapir has lived nearly 30 years in captivity, but in its later years it developed opacity of the cornea and became nearly blind. In the wild it is preyed upon by tigers, which it attempts to dislodge from its back by rushing through the undergrowth and plunging into pools. One which was badly lacerated by a tiger was found by villagers who rescued it and although it was so badly injured that it could not stand up, after being disinfected and hand-fed, it recovered over a period of three months. Occasionally, Malay tapirs damage crops. The gestation period is about 400 days, young weighing 17 lb (7·5 kg) on birth and being black with longitudinal white streaks and spots on the body. These markings disappear in 12 months, and as they disappear the white 'loincloth' appears on the hindquarters. A few tapirs have been noted from the Palembang region, South Sumatra, which lack the white loins and are entirely black except for the white lips and ear-rims. They have been given the subspecific name *T. i. brevetianus,* but it is uncertain whether this is more than just a casual mutation.

The tapirs of Central and South America are all smaller than those of Malaya, more slenderly built, and plain brown, with white tones here and there, but no sharply defined, solid white area. Like the Malay species, however, the young are marked with spots and streaks but at a year old these fade, without being replaced by any adult pattern.

The South American or Brazilian tapir *T. terrestris* is the smallest species and heavy individuals weigh only 400 lb (180 kg). It is plain brown, often with whitish lips and ear-tips, and grey tones on the throat; different races are predominantly black, brown or grey. The top of the head is flat, the midline of the neck is raised and fleshy, and there is a short stiff mane along it. Newborn young weigh only 9 lb (4 kg).

The South American tapir is found throughout the tropical forest and subtropical hardwood forest zones, from Colombia through the Guianas and Brazil into Paraguay and northern Argentina. In the Andes it ascends to about 4,000 ft (1,200 m). It is very similar ecologically to the Malay species, being fond of lowland forest and especially swampy regions. It bathes and wallows a great deal and it walks with its snout close to the ground. The name 'tapir' comes from the Tupi language (Brazilian Indian).

The social life of the South American tapir is unknown. In the San Diego zoo, the captive group forms a structured herd, with dominant and subordinate animals of both sexes. The dominant male and female make what is called the 'sliding squeal', less than a

second in duration. On hearing this sound the others make a 'fluctuating squeal', which is longer and quavers rather than merely decreasing in pitch. This is also uttered when a dominant individual approaches, apparently as an appeasement call and as a sign of pain or fear. Tapirs also utter a challenging snort, and a click made with the tongue and palate, perhaps as a species identification.

Roulin's, Mountain or Woolly tapir *T. pinchaque* is easily distinguishable from the South American by its curly black hair, sometimes over an inch long, and its light cheeks and strongly marked white ear-rims. There is no mane and there are skull differences as well. This species is found in subtropical and temperate forests, wandering into the high grasslands of the Andes, in Colombia, Ecuador, western Venezuela and Peru as far as 6°S. It normally occurs at 9–10,000 ft (2,730–3,040 m), but altitudes as high as 15,000 ft (4,570 m) have been recorded. Even less is known about this species than the others; it is becoming rare, and it is estimated that in Peru at least its numbers have fallen to between 100 and 200.

The last species, the largest of the New World group, is Baird's tapir *T. bairdii,* which weighs 600 lb (270 kg). This species is short-haired like the South American, with very small bristles along the nape as a reduced version of the latter's mane. It is particularly distinguished by its very light, even whitish cheeks, throat and neck, as well as white lips and ear-tips. The head is more convex than the South American or Roulin's tapir, and the nasal bones are supported by an ossification which strengthens the base of the proboscis. This species occurs in South America mainly northwest of the Andes in Ecuador and Colombia, north from the Gulf of Guayaquil. It extends north in Central America through Guatemala and Nicaragua to Veracruz and southeastern Mexico, to the northern limit of the tropical forest. Apparently its invasion into South America has been comparatively recent. Records today indicate a range overlap with the South American tapir in Colombia, which was not recorded previously.

Baird's tapir breeds, in Mexico, in March. The female's oestrus lasts four to five days and during this time the male and female copulate several times. During oestrus the female is very aggressive towards others of her sex, very restless and constantly utters a characteristic squeak. The gestation period is 390–400 days. The young suckle standing, sitting or lying down with equal facility.

Tapirs are virtually defenceless except for their rather thick skins; undoubtedly their shyness and innocuous nature has preserved them, together with their lack of worthwhile 'trophies'. Tapirs are unique, virtual living fossils. FAMILY: Tapiridae, ORDER: Perissodactyla, CLASS: Mammalia. C.P.G.

Large hairy spider of the Tropics popularly called a tarantula.

TARANTULA, scientific name of a genus of tailless *whipscorpions, occurring in the tropical and subtropical regions of North, Central and South America. The popular name 'tarantula' is often used for a group of mygalomorph spiders and although the amblypygids resemble spiders they do not possess spinnerets and their first pair of legs are very long and whip-like. See also Tarantula spiders. ORDER: Amblypygi, CLASS: Arachnida, PHYLUM: Arthropoda.

TARANTULA SPIDERS, popular name originally used for the large *Wolf spider *Lycosa tarantula* of southern Europe, belonging to the suborder Araneomorphae. It gained its name from Taranto in Italy in the 14th century where the strange effects of its bites

were called tarantism. Pain, nausea, partial paralysis and difficulties in breathing responded to no medical treatment. Music accompanied by bouts of wild dancing—the tarantella—over a period of three days were said to bring about a cure. Modern writers know it has a painful bite, but they believe those who suffered the symptoms described above had been bitten by the European Black widow spider *Latrodectus tredecim-guttatus*.

The name tarantula, following American custom, is now used for the unrelated hairy giant spiders which inhabit the tropics throughout the world. These belong to a different suborder, the Mygalomorphae, and to the family Theraphosidae. They eat large insects and small vertebrates so the discovery by early explorers of specimens eating birds led them to be called mygales (bird spiders).

Their bites inflict wounds but the venom seldom has serious effects. They live in tree crevices or holes in the ground and emerge at night. Large insects are their staple diet. The steaming jungles of northern South America produce the largest spiders in the world belonging to such genera as *Lasiodora* and *Grammostola*. They take up to ten years to reach their full size and can survive a further ten years. The body can attain a length of $3\frac{1}{2}$ in (9 cm) and the thick outstretched legs can span 10 in (25 cm).

They are sluggish though capable of rapid darts forward. Tests have shown that limitation to size in spiders is brought about by their respiratory system. A dash lasting seconds can exhaust a huge spider and multiply its heart beats to four times the normal rate.

Although thousands of eggs are laid by each female the mortality amongst the young is high and even when they are full grown their enemies include rodents, parasitic flies and pompilid wasps of the genus *Pepsis*, despite the fact that they have been known to overcome poisonous snakes.

The hairs can cause serious inflammation if they penetrate the human skin or get into the eyes from the fingers. Nevertheless one species in Thailand, *Melopoeus albostriatus*, is collected as a delicacy and eaten after the hairs have been burned off. ORDER: Araneae, CLASS: Arachnida, PHYLUM: Arthropoda.
W.S.B.

TARANTULA DANCING. In the early years of the 19th century a Mr Swinburne was travelling through Italy. He was very keen to see the Tarantella being danced. Although it was too early in the year for the spiders which are the origin of this dance to be about and no one had been bitten, a woman was persuaded to dance. "Up she sprang with a most hideous yell, staggered about the room like a drunken person, holding a handkerchief in both hands, raising them alternately, and moving in very true time. As the music grew brisker, her motions quickened, ... every now and then shrieking very loud. The scene was unpleasant, and, at his (Swinburne's) request, an end was put to it." Swinburne informs us that the room was decorated with bunches of grapes and ribbons and that the dancers were dressed like priestesses of Bacchus. He suggests that Christianity put an end to Bacchanalian rites but that they were being continued under a different guise.

TARDIGRADES, commonly called Water bears or Moss bears, are minute animals, mostly about $\frac{1}{50}$ in (0·5 mm) in length. The body is cylindrical and the adult has four pairs of stumpy legs. Each leg bears one or more claws; the largest number of claws being found in the marine species *Echiniscoides sigismundi*, which has eight claws on each leg. The head is short and broad, and bears a narrow mouth through which small needle like stylets can be protruded. These are used to pierce plant cells, from which the contents are sucked out by means of a muscular pump in the first part of the gut. A few tardigrades have become predators and prey upon other tardigrades, nematodes and rotifers.

The body wall of a tardigrade is often translucent, but it may also be armed with opaque plates and spines. Most are colourless, however, but a few are coloured bright red with carotenoid pigments, and in some species the green colour of the food in the gut can be seen through the body wall. There is no heart or circulatory system, but there is a

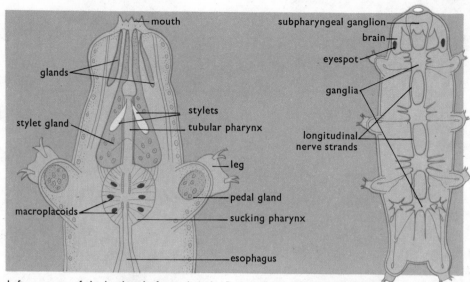

Left: anatomy of the head end of a tardigrade. Right: nervous system of the same.

nervous system based on the annelid-arthropod plan, with a cerebral ganglion, or brain, and a short chain of ganglia under the gut.

The sexes are separate, and the male may practise hypodermal impregnation. This means that the sperms are injected into the body cavity of the female from any point on the surface of her body. The sperms then make their way to the ovary where they fertilize the ripe eggs, which are provided with a tough outer coat before being laid. On hatching the young tardigrade resembles the adult in general form, but has only two pairs of legs.

The majority of tardigrades are dwellers in moss, and this habit exposes them to the danger of desiccation. During the summer the moss may become completely dry, so the tardigrades need some means of surviving drought. They have developed a remarkable capacity to suspend active life and allow themselves to dry with the moss, shrivelling as they lose water. When in the dried state they can withstand such extreme conditions as being placed in liquid air or kept in dryness over such powerful desiccants as phosphorus pentoxide which removes all trace of water vapour from the air. It is a remarkable sight to watch a shrivelled tardigrade swell up and gradually resume normal activity when water is added.

Some tardigrades are truly aquatic. Among the marine forms there are several that live in peculiar habitats. *Echiniscoides sigismundi* for instance is often found in the crevices of the shells of barnacles on the seashore, but it has also been found crawling about in the mantle cavity of the Common mussel *Mytilus edulis*. *Batillipes mirus* lives among sand grains in shallow water, and has disc-like expansions on the ends of its claws, which help it to cling to the sand grains. *Tetrakentron synaptae* has been found associated with tentacles around the mouth of

the sand dwelling Sea cucumber *Leptosynapta galliennei*, and finally *Pleocola limnoriae* has been found living on the surface of the wood boring isopod *Limnoria lignorum*.

Among the other aquatic species perhaps the most remarkable is *Thermozodium esakii*, which lives in a sulphurous thermal spring in Japan, where the temperature of the water reaches 106°F (41°C).

In old classifications the tardigrades were often placed among the arachnids, because they have eight legs, but modern classifications place them in a group of their own, near the *Onychophora. CLASS: Tardigrada, PHYLUM: Arthropoda.
Jo.G.

TARPAN *Equus przewalskii silvaticus* and *E. p. gmelini*, true wild horses which lived in Europe and western Asia before being exterminated during the last two centuries. FAMILY: Equidae, ORDER: Perissodactyla, CLASS: Mammalia. For further details see horse.

TARPONS, powerful, silvery fishes related to the tenpounders. They are strong swimmers and are renowned for their fighting powers when hooked. There are two species, the Atlantic tarpon *Tarpon atlanticus* and the Indo-Pacific tarpon *Megalops cyprinoides*. The two are outwardly so similar that many authors place them in the same genus. Recent studies have shown, however, that there are fundamental differences in the skull which suggest that the two tarpons are very different fishes. The body is fairly compressed with large silvery scales and there is a single dorsal fin with the last ray prolonged into a filament. Although primarily marine, the tarpons are not infrequently found in freshwater and sometimes even in foul waters. The Indo-Pacific tarpon reaches 3 ft (90 cm) in length, but the Atlantic tarpon is a huge fish, growing to 8 ft (2·4 m) and weighing up to 300 lb (135 kg). Like the ladyfish and the tenpounder, the tarpons begin life as a ribbon-like lepto-cephalus larva resembling that of the eels. FAMILY: Megalopidae, ORDER: Elopiformes, CLASS: Pisces.

TARSIER, a peculiar nocturnal mammal related to lemurs and also to monkeys, apes and man as indicated by its large, forward-directed eyes, its opposable thumb and big toe and its relatively large brain. It is about the size of a rat, with a head and body length of about 5 in (13 cm) and a tail 8 in (20 cm) long, remarkable for being hairless apart from the tip, which has a feather-like arrangement of fine hairs. The tarsier always rests and jumps in a vertical position, typically moving around in bushes and high grass. It can rotate its head through a half-circle and, like an owl, look directly backwards over its shoulder, in order to sight a suitable landing-point for its next jump.

The tarsier ranges over the Malay Archipelago, from Sumatra to Borneo, Celebes and the Philippines. There are three species: the Philippine tarsier *Tarsius syrichta,* the Spectral tarsier *T. spectrum,* of Celebes and neighbouring islands, and Horsfield's tarsier *T. bancanus,* of Sumatra and Borneo. All are mainly insectivorous, but eat some fruits. FAMILY: Tarsiidae, SUBORDER: Prosimii, ORDER: Primates, CLASS: Mammalia.

TARSUS, the bones of the vertebrate ankle. The bones of the foot comprise the metatarsus. In birds, the term 'tarsus' has a special connotation, for the tarsal bones proper are elongated and fused with each other and with certain of the metatarsal bones to form a single unit properly called the 'tarso-metatarsus' but commonly known as the 'tarsus'. This gives the bird an extra section in the leg—the one above the foot—resulting in more efficient locomotion on the ground.

TASMANIAN DEVIL *Sarcophilus harrisii,* a carnivorous marsupial included in the family Dasyuridae which also includes the Native cats, Banded anteater and Marsupial wolf. The Tasmanian devil is a fox-terrier-sized animal of powerful build with a widely gaping mouth and strong teeth. The muzzle is short and broad and the ears short and rounded. The head and body are about 28 in (70 cm) and the tail about 12 in (30 cm) long. There are five toes on the forefeet and four on the hindfeet each with a strong claw. The general body colour is black but there is a white band across the chest and sometimes a white band across the rump.

The jaw gape of the Tasmanian devil is wide and the teeth are large and strong. As in other dasyurid marsupials there are four

Philippine tarsier, remarkable for its large eyes, one of three species of primitive relatives of monkeys, apes and man.

upper and three lower incisor teeth. The canine teeth are powerful and the premolars sharp and reduced to two in each jaw. The four molar teeth of the upper jaw bite only partly on the four lower molars, a powerful crushing action being obtained by the uppers sliding past to the outside of the lower molars.

The Tasmanian devil is now confined to Tasmania where it has been described as rare. Recent studies have, however, shown it to be very abundant over at least some of its former range and it has been implicated in the killing of some domestic animals. Local eradication or control measures are sometimes undertaken. Tasmania is, however, but a remnant of the former range of the animal. It occurred in the Northern Territory of Australia, at about 12°S latitude, 3,000 years ago, in various other parts of Australia at about the same time and during the Pleistocene epoch. In Victoria, Australia, at about 38°S latitude, it was present five to seven hundred years ago.

The Tasmanian devil is a, usually, solitary, terrestrial, nocturnal, carnivore which feeds on mammals and birds, a variety of insects and invertebrate animals and on carrion. The litter size is up to four and the young are born in the autumn of each year. FAMILY: Dasyuridae, ORDER: Marsupialia, CLASS: Mammalia.
G.B.S.

TASMANIAN WOLF *Thylacinus cynocephalus,* also called thylacine or *Marsupial wolf, the largest carnivorous marsupial, once numerous over most of the continent of Australia but persecuted to the point of extinction. It now probably only survives in the wilder regions of western Tasmania.

TASTE, a form of chemoreception, or chemical sense, carried on within the buccal, or mouth, cavity. In mammals the receptors are the taste buds found mainly on the tongue. There appear to be four main primary taste sensations: sweet, sour, bitter and salt and possibly two others, alkaline and metallic as well. In 'tasting' food these are combined with information from the sense of smell, also a chemical sense, to give a greater variety of sensations.

In aquatic forms such as fishes 'taste' receptors may be present elsewhere, such as on barbels or even scattered over the general body surface.

TAXIS, a kind of behaviour concerned with the orientation of an animal, enabling it to maintain a fixed position with regard to a source of stimulation. In the widest sense this includes the action of a chameleon turning towards its prey to aim and the movement of a hoverfly towards a light source in a darkened room. Since to be effective most behaviour must be directed in a particular way, e.g. a predator to its prey or a male towards a female, the taxis component is an important part of any behaviour pattern.

Usually represented as highly ferocious, the Tasmanian devil it seems looks more dangerous than it is.

A great deal of attention has been paid to the orientation behaviour of invertebrate animals and as a result a number of different kinds of taxes have been described. At the same time it has been possible at least to indicate how animals, like flies, beetles or flatworms, find their way, for example, to a light or to food.

A blowfly larva on a table-top in a darkened room will move away from a light source, crawling straight down the beam. In nature this response to light causes the older larvae to crawl away from their feeding places and go into some crack or down into the soil where they will pupate in safety. On examination the larva can be observed to move by looping movements during which it swings its head-end from side to side. If the light is arranged so that the larva's head-end is illuminated every time it swings to the left, the larva reacts each time by swinging violently to the right with the result that it moves round in a circle. This shows that when it is crawling in the light beam the insect bends to left and right comparing the illumination which falls on each side of its head as it turns. If it is more strongly lit to one side, it will swing more violently and turn until its head is equally illuminated on both sides. Because the animal bends to one side and then to the other, behaviour of this sort is called klinotaxis. A planarian worm uses the same kind of behaviour to find a piece of food but, instead of responding to light, it uses sense organs sensitive to the chemicals diffusing from the food. By swinging its head to right and left it senses whether it is moving up the gradient of concentration of the chemical to the food.

But a number of invertebrates manage to make their way to or from a light without casting from side to side as an animal showing a klinotaxis does. An adult hoverfly set down in a light beam will move up the beam towards the light source, but if one eye is covered, the fly moves in circles turning towards the side with the uncovered eye. This suggests that the animal steers itself by using both eyes and moving so that each is equally illuminated. And indeed this idea is supported by the fly's behaviour if it is put down in front of, but midway between, two lights of equal intensity, for it moves forward travelling between the lights on a path at an equal distance from each. On the other hand, if one of the lights is twice as strong as the other, it chooses a path which is always twice as far from the stronger light than it is from the weaker. Again, the illumination falling on the two eyes is balanced. This kind of orientation, which involves the simultaneous comparison of the stimulation of two sense organs, is tropotaxis.

A honeybee will behave similarly to the hoverfly in a beam of light, but when one eye is covered the bee can still make its way to the light source along a straight path. It must, therefore, be able to orientate using one eye alone. This is telotaxis. It is brought about by a different response of different parts of the eye to illumination. Take the right eye as an example; if the area of it which faces towards the rear is lit the animal turns strongly to the right—which has the effect of bringing it round to face the light. If, however, it is illuminated on the median front part of the eye, where the ommatidia face a little to the left, the turn will be to the left, but less strong. Just beside this small median area is a group of ommatidia (see eye) which point forward and light falling on this area evokes only forward movement for the animal is then pointed at the source. Light response of this sort is called a phototaxis. It is apparently the way in which, for example, winkles on the shore maintain their position, keeping in roughly the same ecological zone. When the tide goes down, a winkle sets off on a feeding excursion moving towards the sun for a time and then reversing this response to travel away from it. As a result the winkle comes back to approximately the place from which it set out.

Taxes are the behaviours by which animals orientate themselves at fixed angles to

the source of stimulation. This angle will be 0° if it moves to the source, or 180°, if it moves away. It may also move at other angles. When carrying out a *dorsal light reaction an animal orientates itself so that its body is at 90° to the direction of the incident light, in other words, this is a form of taxis. Indeed it is a special case of a light-compass reaction, for when animals show this reaction they may move with the incident light at any angle to them, the angle being temporarily fixed.

A number of animals—bees, ants and pigeons are only a few of them—use objects in their surroundings as landmarks for guidance. This has been called pharotaxis. The landmarks are learned and used for orientation subsequently. In fact, young ants on first leaving the nest simply run towards the sun, find food and reverse their phototactic response to bring them back. These excursions are over short distances only. As they become more experienced they begin to go farther and in other directions, using a light-compass orientation. Finally they learn to depend on landmarks and the polarized light pattern in the sky.

Taxes may involve other stimuli than light as has already been mentioned. A planarian worm uses chemotaxis to find its food (to give the behaviour its full name: chemoklinotaxis). Responses to currents in wind or water may direct animals upwind or upstream; this is rheotaxis. While reaction to touch which leads animals to push themselves into narrow cracks where contact on their body is at a maximum is thigmotaxis. See orientation and navigation.   J.D.C.

TAYRA *Eira barbara*, a South American forest-dwelling member of the weasel family (Mustelidae) renowned for its swiftness and climbing ability. The single species is distributed over southern Mexico south to Argentina and Paraguay. Tayras have relatively long, slender legs and tails which set them apart from the other, usually short-legged, mustelids. The very short, coarse fur is sepia or black, save for the brown head and light yellow throat or chest patch which may be speckled with white. Individuals with an overall buff colouration have been reported occasionally. The broad head with flat, rounded ears has such a human resemblance that Mexicans refer to the tayra as 'cabeza de viejo' (head of an old man) and the subspecific name is appropriately *senilis*. Adult males are markedly larger and more muscular than females. Consequently, overall length varies from 38·5 – 45·3 in (98 – 115 cm), of which the tail accounts for at least 16 in (40 cm), and the weight varies from 9 – 13 lb (4·2 – 5·8 kg).

Like the marten or fisher, tayras are equally at home in trees as on the ground and have often been observed in the wild chasing each other in the loftiest tree tops. This marked arboreal tendency allows them to quickly out-distance such terrestrial predators as man or dog. The strong, non-

The taxes (singular, taxis) exhibited by *Amoeba*.

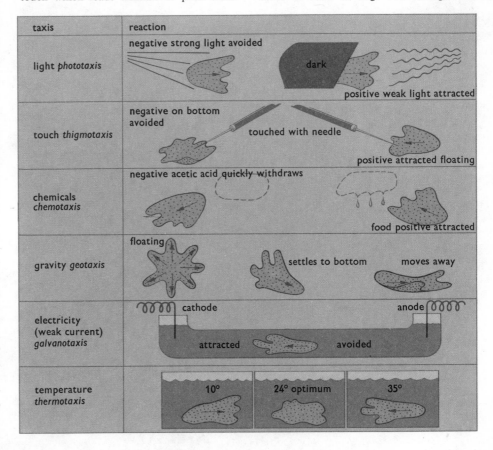

taxis	reaction		
light *phototaxis*	negative strong light avoided	dark	positive weak light attracted
touch *thigmotaxis*	negative on bottom avoided	touched with needle	positive attracted floating
chemicals *chemotaxis*	negative acetic acid quickly withdraws		food positive attracted
gravity *geotaxis*	floating	settles to bottom	moves away
electricity (weak current) *galvanotaxis*	cathode — attracted		anode — avoided
temperature *thermotaxis*	10°	24° optimum	35°

retractile claws and naked soles are great assets in climbing and, although the tail is not prehensile, it serves as a balancer. Tayras share with the coati *Nasua* spp, which lives in the same environment, a similar hand over hand method of ascent and likewise when descending head first, the feet are turned backwards, grasping the bark. On the ground, the normal gait is a trot but when playing or pursued tayras gallop and jump with surprising speed and agility. Usually solitary, sometimes living in small family groups with the subadult young, this species is active during the cooler parts of the day, becoming nocturnal where they are disturbed. Hollow trees, bushes or high branches serve as shelter or resting spots for brief naps during the day. The male tayra scent-marks when passing over certain branches, hardly breaking stride to squat and briefly drag his anal glands over the chosen surface. In common with other arboreal carnivores, the tayra does not set aside a particular spot for its toilet activities and may defaecate either on the ground or in the trees.

Wild tayras have been frequently seen eating bananas and fallen cecropia fruit but they also prey on a variety of animals such as Tree squirrels, agoutis, Mouse opossums, snakes and birds, which are swiftly dispatched with a neck-bite and a shake of the head. When chasing a victim, a tayra may swim but does not do so willingly. The precise length of the gestation period is not known, two to four cubs have been found, however, in makeshift grass nests in May. The young, blind and helpless at birth, are covered in sparse black fur, the brown head fur appearing only six months later. Natives claim that the tayra's baculum contains certain aphrodisiac properties, a notion probably arising from its human appearance and the large size of the male's external genitalia. FAMILY: Mustelidae, ORDER: Carnivora, CLASS: Mammalia.   N.D.

TEETH, the name given to a wide variety af hard structures found in and around the buccal (mouth) cavity and elsewhere in animals. See dentition.

TEGU *Tupinambis nigropunctatus,* one of the largest of the lizards in the family Teiidae, an inhabitant of tropical South America, is about 3 ft (1 m) long. It is terrestrial and lays its eggs in the large spherical nests of certain termites. It is omnivorous and disliked for its tendency to take chicks and eggs around farms. The bulk of its diet, however, consists of frogs, insects, other lizards, and even leaves and soft fruits. FAMILY: Teiidae, ORDER: Squamata, CLASS: Reptilia.

Opposite page: the tayra, a South American member of the weasel family.

TEIIDS, a family of lizard-like reptiles, related to Old World lizards and skinks, with a long tail and a long, narrow, deeply-cleft tongue. Although the front teeth are conical, as is usual in lizards, the lateral teeth of both jaws may assume several different forms according to the species, depending on the feeding habits. For example, the Caiman lizard *Dracaena guianensis* has conical front teeth followed by large, oval teeth adapted for crushing snail shells. The skin of teiids is armed only with superficial epidermal scales; scales of the type present in the dermal layer of the skin of some related families being absent.

The Caiman lizard is unusual among the teiids in being semi-aquatic as most species are definitely terrestrial, arboreal or fossorial. The larger teiids have a tendency to be more active in daylight, whereas the smaller species are largely nocturnal.

The 40 genera are restricted to the American continent, mainly south of Mexico, where they occupy a position corresponding to that of the lizard family Lacertidae in the Old World. Only the genus *Cnemidophorus* reaches as far north as the United States.

The larger species of teiids, known as tegus, may attain a length of nearly 4 ft (122 cm) and superficially resemble Monitor lizards (Varanidae). The Black tegu *Tupinambis teguixin* and the Golden tegu *T. nigropunctatus* range over much of Central and South America but the Red tegu *T. rufescens* is mostly restricted to Argentina.

Ameivas are small, attractively marked teiids which resemble the smaller European lizards in general behaviour and form. The Jungle runner or Surinam lizard *Ameiva ameiva* and the South American Striped lizard *A. undulatus* are common and widely distributed species of ameivas which may attain a maximum length of 18 in (46 cm) but are generally considerably smaller.

The life histories of teiids are not well known. The Coastal whiptail *Cnemidophorus tigris,* which extends northwards into the United States, has been observed to mate several times between May and July and lay several egg batches per season. The incubation period for this species is about 80 days in the United States.

Teiids are mostly carnivorous. In captivity they will feed on insects, lizards, birds, mice and carrion. Some species will also take eggs and fruit, and it has been reported that tegus will drink blood, milk and lemonade as well as water. FAMILY: Teiidae, ORDER: Squamata, CLASS: Reptilia.   M.J.P.

TELEOSTS or modern bony fishes, the group that contains the overwhelming majority of living fishes. At least 20,000 different species are known, inhabiting every sea, lake and river in the world. In the classification adopted here, the teleosts have been grouped into 30 orders containing forms as diverse as perches, eels, seahorses, flounders, anglerfishes and boxfishes. See fishes. INFRACLASS: Teleostei, SUBCLASS: Actinopterygii, CLASS: Pisces.

TELESCOPE-EYES, deep-sea fishes with tubular eyes of the family Giganturidae and distantly related to the whalefishes. They are also called giant-tails. These fishes have cylindrical bodies and reach 9 in (23 cm) in length. The body is naked, the pectoral fins are set behind the head and very high up on the flanks and the lower lobe of the tail is

In the rare and curious oceanic fish *Opisthoproctus soleatus* the telescopic eyes are directed upwards and cannot be turned in any other direction.

mouth

gill opening

elongated into a long banner. They live in all oceans at depths down to 12,000 ft (3,600 m). The tubular eyes give these fishes excellent binocular vision, an attribute that is rare in fishes but one that enables them to make accurate estimates of distances when pouncing on prey. Like many deep-sea fishes, the telescope-eyes have elastic stomachs and are capable of swallowing fishes larger than themselves.

Gigantura is a relatively solid looking fish and is unusual amongst deep-sea forms in having a silvery body. Its relative, the Pacific Telescope-eye fish *Bathyleptus lisae,* is much more fragile in appearance but both fishes have long, fang-like teeth. Almost nothing is known of the biology of these fishes and only about 12 specimens of *Bathyleptus* have ever been caught. FAMILY: Giganturidae, ORDER: Cetomimiformes, CLASS: Pisces.

TELLIN SHELLS, marine bivalve molluscs, also called Sunset shells, are found throughout the Atlantic and other parts of the world. Most have a round or elongated shell rather like the *Venus shells. They also have a deep pallial sinus and in the majority of species the lower part of the sinus mark on the inside of the shell is joined to the pallial line. This is a diagnostic feature of this group.

Most tellins are unisexual, that is they are either male or female. This is sometimes difficult to demonstrate as many of the bivalves are consecutive hermaphrodites producing first male and female gametes. They are very successful at colonizing brackish water and can tolerate quite large changes in salinity. The Baltic tellin *Macoma balthica* is found in the near freshwater Baltic Sea and in estuaries in similar habitats to another tellin, the Peppery furrow shell *Scrobicularia plana*. Both of these animals develop huge numbers in these situations, populations of the Peppery furrow shell of 1,094 per m^2 have been estimated in the Tamar Estuary and 5,900 per m^2 for the Baltic tellin in the Mersey. These large populations reflect the abundance of food for detritus feeders in this estuarine habitat.

Within the Tellinacea those animals with large gills have small labial palps and individuals with small gills have large palps. The palps of bivalves are normally considered to be ciliated sorting areas where food is finally selected for ingestion and this inverse relationship seems to suggest that the gills may play some active part in this sorting. The food is taken into the gut as particles embedded in a mucus rope which are then crushed in the stomach between the crystalline style and the hard gastric shield, a system which works like a pestle and mortar.

The tellins have long groping siphons which are used to search for food lying on the surface of the substrate. This method of collection is unusual in the bivalves as most filter suspended plankton from water drawn into the mantle cavity to ventilate the gills. As the searching for food is such an important aspect in the life of this group one might expect they would have evolved efficient methods for the systematic searching of the area within the immediate vicinity of their burrows within reach of their siphons. This would imply some 'awareness' on the part of the animal as to the exact degree of extension of the siphons at any one time. All the tellins search the sand systematically producing a circular mark in the sand. There is a special sense organ, a proprioreceptor, in the cruciform muscle at the base of the siphons, which gives information about the degree of extension of the siphons. This receptor would also give the necessary information to the animal to enable it to coordinate the withdrawal of its siphons and the closing of its valves, as would have to occur if it was being attacked by a predator. If such information were lacking one could imagine the valves closing and trapping the partially extended siphons outside the shell.

The foot of these animals is broad and triangular in outline. They burrow by inserting the foot which is anchored by its large surface area, and not by expansion as in the *Venus shells, and then contracting the muscles in the foot. Often shells lie on one side in the sand when feeding. All can move very quickly laterally through the sand and are also able to bury themselves when exposed on the surface. FAMILY: Tellinacea, ORDER: Eulamellibranchia, CLASS: Bivalvia, PHYLUM: Mollusca.   P.F.N.

TEMPERATURE REGULATION, process of control over the rate at which the body gains and loses heat. There is one main reason why the temperature of animals is so important and that is because basically they are biochemical machines. They do not obtain energy from physical sources such as the pendulums and springs of clocks. Instead they are activated by chemical reactions and chemical reactions are very sensitive to changes in temperature (see Q_{10}). It is claimed that if you time ants walking along a measuring stick you can show that their speed is doubled for every 10°F (5·6°C) rise in temperature and by timing enough of them you can determine the temperature to within one degree. It is apparent, therefore, that animals are much more active if they can be kept warm. Futhermore, since all animals produce heat, particularly when they move, it would be easy to keep animals more active simply by insulating them so that they retained this heat. Suppose we did this to a man by placing him in a large insulated flask of the sort used to keep drinks warm. Would he get progressively more and more active? Unfortunately, no. A man at rest produces about 2,000 kilocalories of heat per day, i.e. enough heat to raise the temperature of 100 kg of water by 20°C. A man normally weighs a little less than 100 kg and so his temperature would rise by about 2°F (1°C) per hour and he would be dead within about five hours.

These then are the reasons why temperature regulation is so important. If animals can keep warm they are more active than when their body temperature falls but if they get overheated, death occurs. Obviously, therefore, temperature regulation must involve ways, not only of keeping the animal warm, but also of cooling it so that its temperature does not rise too high. These requirements are rather stringent and only birds and mammals have perfected the mechanisms of temperature regulation. They are therefore called homoiotherms, i.e. capable of maintaining a constant temperature or warm-blooded as opposed to other animals which are poikilotherms, i.e. having a body temperature that varies with that of their surroundings, usually called cold-blooded.

The adaptations of homoiotherms may be considered as of two types; those which enable the animals to raise their temperature and those which they use to lower their temperature. In both cases, however, the brain appears to play a major role in responding to the temperature of the blood and initiating the responses which regulate the temperature of the animal.

The main source of heat for homoiotherms is their own metabolism. The chemical reactions which are continually occurring to release energy in the animal also release heat which warms up the animal's body. Since these chemical reactions are common to all animals, however, it is difficult to see why some animals are

Poikilotherms tend to cool down when outside temperatures fall, whereas homoiotherms like birds and mammals maintain a constant body temperature.

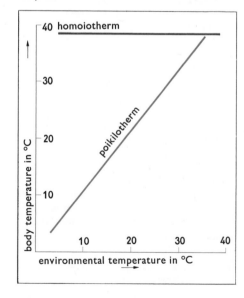

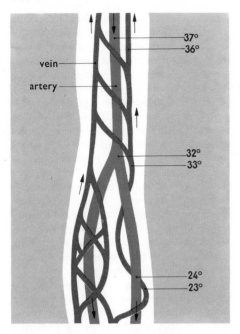

Countercurrent system in the human arm. Cold venous blood (blue) passes close to warm arterial blood (red), removing heat before it can reach the colder parts of the body.

Indicated in brown are the fat deposits (known as 'brown fat') in a new-born rabbit. These act as a sort of 'electric blanket'.

warm-blooded and others cold-blooded. The explanation appears to be that birds and mammals generally produce more heat than for example fishes, amphibians and reptiles. It is difficult to get figures to substantiate this because to be accurate measurements of heat production in different animals should be obtained at the same temperature and 98·6°F (37°C) which is approximately the body temperature of most large mammals is lethal to many animals such as fishes and frogs. Snakes and alligators survive these conditions quite well, however, and it can be shown that at these temperatures reptiles have a heat production of only about a quarter of that of a man of the same body weight. Furthermore, when the reptile's temperature falls again so does its rate of heat production whereas the opposite situation holds for mammals and birds. The increased heat production of cooled homoiotherms is due to the contraction of small or large groups of muscles—shivering. This increases the heat production of the animal and counteracts its tendency to cool.

The outer surfaces of the bodies of most warm-blooded animals are covered in either hair or feathers. Both of these structures can trap a layer of air over the outside of the body and since air is a good insulator, it reduces the amount of heat lost from the skin. When these animals tend to cool, the brain sends impulses down the nerves to the skin causing the muscles at the bases of the hairs and feathers to contract. This lifts these

structures off the surface of the skin and so increases the thickness of the layer of trapped air and hence the insulation around the body. The effectiveness of this mechanism has been demonstrated in the wren *Troglodytes aedon* which can normally survive at a temperature of 27°F (−3°C). If the bird is put in a very small box which prevents it from fluffing out its feathers, it can only tolerate 50°F (10°C). In the human, a similar mechanism still operates even though we have very little hair over our bodies. Thus in the cold we produce 'goose pimples' as the tiny muscles at the bases of the hairs pull on the skin and cause it to be dimpled. The hairs are so small, however, that they have little effect upon temperature regulation and most of the insulation against the loss of heat from our bodies is due to a layer of fat immediately below the skin. A similar phenomenon is seen in the aquatic whale

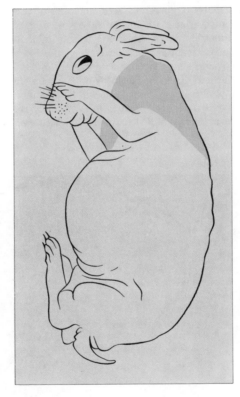

where there is a thick layer of blubber beneath the virtually hairless surface of the animal. The quantity of heat which is lost from the body can also be reduced by constricting the blood vessels in the outer layers of the skin so that the warm blood is then diverted to the deeper blood vessels beneath the fat. Thus, our hands 'turn blue with cold' as the red blood is diverted away from the outermost layers; reducing to one-hundredth the circulation of blood through these cold regions. The mechanism, is, in fact, so effective at reducing the loss of heat from the skin that the temperature in the deeper parts of the body may actually rise by 1°F (0·5°C)

when man is in a cold environment.

There is one final method of preventing excessive heat loss which is often found in warm-blooded animals. This is the so-called counter-current system of blood flow which is found in the limbs of many birds and mammals which live in cold environments. In a counter-current system the cold venous blood returning from an arm passes close to an artery carrying warm blood to the ends of the limb. The warm blood is thus cooled down before it enters the colder part of the hand while the venous blood is warmed up before it re-enters the main mass of the body. This system keeps the heat in the body and stops it being lost from the more exposed limbs. Counter-current blood systems are frequently found in the feet of water birds and the flippers of aquatic mammals and in the long limbs of wading birds.

These mechanisms effectively keep the body temperature of birds and mammals from falling. In hot climates, however, the problem is usually to stop the body from overheating and the same difficulty may be found even in cold climates when animals exercise vigorously. Heat must then be lost from the body surface as fast as it is produced and this is facilitated by flattening the hairs and feathers, so as to reduce their insulating effect, and by dilating the blood vessels in the exposed parts of the skin. In many birds and mammals the skin is only exposed over the face and feet and these are therefore particularly important sites for heat loss. The Laysan albatross *Diomedia immutabilis,* for example, attempts to cool itself by holding its feet off the hot earth thus radiating heat from the exposed web of skin. The Wood stork *Mycteria americana* has a similar cooling problem when it is nesting in exposed sites at the tops of trees. In this case, however, it is difficult to radiate heat from the feet since they contain a countercurrent heat exchanger which as we have already mentioned retains the heat in the body. This prevents excessive heat loss by the stork when it is fishing with its legs submerged in cold water but tends to make the bird overheat when it is nesting. Under these circumstances the bird will frequently urinate upon its legs and this produces some heat loss through the evaporation of water.

The evaporation of water from the body is in fact the other main way in which animals can cool themselves. It takes 576 calories of heat to evaporate 1 gram of water and this quantity of heat is therefore removed from the evaporating surface during this process. The skin and lungs are both permeable to water which is therefore continually evaporating from these sites and cooling the animal. In man, about equal volumes of water are lost from each of these sites and since this loss of water cannot be controlled it is called 'insensible perspiration'. This is to distinguish it from sensible perspiration which is the water secreted from the sweat glands in the skin when the animal gets overheated. Sweat glands are well-developed in man (where there are about 2,500,000) and the horse but most mammals have relatively few and birds have none. In these animals the evaporation of water is still used as a cooling device but the water is evaporated from, for example, the tongue in dogs and from the lungs and respiratory system by panting. It is perhaps difficult to imagine how important the evaporation of water is in temperature regulation. It was, however, clearly demonstrated as long ago as 1798 by Blagden, a Secretary of the Royal Society. He went into a room heated to 260°F (126°C) i.e. well above the boiling point of water and stayed there for $\frac{3}{4}$ hour without harmful effects although a beef steak which he took with him not only cooked but baked until it was quite hard. He could not have done this if the room had been humid for he was only able to keep his body temperature normal by evaporating sweat and water from his skin and lungs and was no doubt very thirsty when he finished the experiment.

It is easy to understand, therefore, why deserts are such inhospitable environments for not only can they be very hot but they are also short of water and desert animals have evolved their own methods of dealing with these problems. Some live in burrows to avoid the heat of the day. In other animals, such as the camel the body temperature fluctuates so that it falls during the cold night and then slowly rises again during the day. Thus, the animal does not have to sweat to avoid overheating until quite late in the day. The camel also has quite a thick layer of fur on its back for this can protect an animal from heating up just as well as it can insulate it from cooling down.

Other animals have also ceased to maintain their body temperatures within the normal narrow range. Thus, some mammals (e.g. bats, hedgehogs) and birds (e.g. hummingbirds) hibernate at certain times and their body temperatures fall. They usually still regulate their temperature, however, although at a much lower level by some of the mechanisms that have already been discussed. Many hibernating mammals also have a tissue known as brown fat which is capable of liberating large quantities of heat and warming the animal up at the time of arousal from hibernation. This is particularly interesting since newborn mammals are generally very poor at temperature regulating and these same deposits of brown fat are found in these animals. It will be apparent that temperature regulation involves control over the rate at which animals gain heat and the rate at which they lose it. K.S.

TENCH *Tinca tinca,* perhaps the most easily identified of all the carp-like fishes of European freshwaters. It is a stocky fish with very small scales, heavy and rounded fins and a body that is dark olive-green shot with gold. The belly is light grey or reddish grey with a violet sheen. One variety is green shot with gold with the mouth red. The tench, usually a rather sluggish fish, spends most of its time on the bottom rooting around the mud in ponds or slow-flowing waters. It hides away in winter, sometimes in the company of other tenches, almost in a state of hibernation but it will stir on very warm days. A really large tench can weigh up to 10 lb (4·5 kg) and any angler who has caught these large fishes will vouch for the fact that they can be anything but sluggish. When hooked their lethargy disappears as if by magic.

Old legends refer to the tench as the doctorfish because of its alleged habit of allowing injured fishes to rub their wounds on its healing slime. These healing properties were supposed to confer some kind of immunity from attack on the tench, but this is certainly not true since both perch and pike will readily eat this fish. The tench is also reputed to remove leeches from carp in much the same way as the Cleaner fishes remove parasites from other and larger species. FAMILY: Cyprinidae, ORDER: Cypriniformes, CLASS: Pisces.

Tench, or doctorfish, European carp credited with healing properties.

TENPOUNDER, the name given to the various species of *Elops,* silvery marine fishes somewhat resembling the herring. The tenpounder is now recognized as being related, not to the herring-like fishes, but surprisingly to the eels, these two outwardly dissimilar groups being united by the possession of ribbon-like leptocephalus larvae which later metamorphose into small replicas of the adult. The tenpounder is a slender fish with many small and silvery scales and a single soft-rayed dorsal fin. It shows several very primitive characters, such as the very high number of bony plates (branchiostegal rays) which support the gill membranes, the presence of teeth along the parasphenoid on the roof of the mouth, and the presence of gular plates or paired plate-like bones under the lower jaw (see fishes).

The tenpounders are found in all tropical seas. They live in coastal waters and grow to over 3 ft (90 cm) in length. In the United States the fish is called the tenpounder or bonefish; in South Africa it is the springer (because it leaps when hooked) or Cape salmon; and in Australia it is the Giant herring or bananafish. This well demonstrates the confusion that can arise when an animal is referred to solely by its common name. FAMILY: Elopidae, ORDER: Elopiformes, CLASS: Pisces.

TENRECS, related to moles and shrews but possessing many primitive characters and having several dental and osteological features reminiscent of certain marsupials. They are an ancient group and probably reached their present stronghold in Madagascar as far back as the Cretaceous period. During their long isolation on this island, the tenrecs have undergone notable *adaptive radiation, evolving different forms to fill many ecological niches, just as the marsupials have done in Australia. Half the genera have spines, and *Setifer* and *Echinops* closely resemble hedgehogs. *Oryzorictes* has developed fossorial habits and anatomical adaptations. *Limnogale* is semi-aquatic and *Microgale* parallels the shrews in its way of life.

The tenrecs formerly lived on mainland Africa and are regarded as closely related to *Potamogale,* the Otter shrew. Indeed, this animal is often included in the Tenrecidae. Tenrecs are also considered to be close relatives of the West Indian solenodon, despite their enormous geographical separation.

Tenrecs range in size from only 2 in (5 cm) long up to rabbit-sized species of 16 in (40 cm) in length. Some are tailless, but *Microgale* has a very long tail supported by 47 vertebrae, more than in any other mammal, apart from some of the pangolins. The skull is narrow and long (especially the nasal

part), but is not constricted in the orbital region. Many tenrecs have spiny skins, but are unable to roll up into a spiny ball as effectively as the hedgehogs because their skin musculature is less well developed.

They are found in Madagascar and the adjacent Comoro Islands, where they inhabit a variety of biotopes including montane forests, grassland, scrub and marshes. Most live in burrows and are either crepuscular or nocturnal. They are basically terrestrial animals, feeding on a variety of plant and animal foods, but mainly on ground-dwelling invertebrates. *Tenrec* hibernates in the cold dry season, but *Hemicentetes,* at least, is

active all the year round. Some tenrecs are among the most prolific of mammals, rivalling even the rodents in having up to 25 young per litter. Some of the larger species of tenrec are hunted by the local people as a source of food.

There are ten genera of tenrecs (with about 20 species). Some of the described forms are exceedingly rare and virtually nothing is known about them. *Cryptogale* for instance is known only from a single broken skull. *Dasogale* resembles *Setifer,* but again is only known from the type specimen. *Geogale* is a small mouse-like species, very rare and little known. The main types of

A Hedgehog tenrec of Madagascar.

Portion of a sandy shore where thousands of tubes made by the terebellid worm *Lanice conchilega* project 2–5 cm above the gravel.

tenrec are reviewed below, the first three having spines and the remainder being without.

1 Common tenrec *Tenrec*: a fairly large species, 14 in (35 cm) long, with small eyes, triangular ears and no tail. The grey-brown coat consists of stiff bristles and thin spines. They live in dry bush country and accumulate fat during the summer and hibernate in special burrows during the southern winter (May–October). They mate soon after hibernation ends, and produce 20 or more young in a litter. The young remain in a family group for several weeks during nocturnal feeding forays.

2 Striped tenrec *Hemicentetes*: a rat-sized animal considered to be similar in form to the ancestral tenrec. It is covered with black hair, with longitudinal bands of yellow spines forming stripes along the body. The spines can be erected but the animal does not roll up and rely on them for defence. *Hemicentetes* is active day and night, burrows, but does not hibernate.

3 Hedgehog tenrecs *Setifer echinops*: tiny animals resembling hedgehogs, these are especially common on higher ground. The spines are interspersed with soft white hair, and even extend down on to the tail. They roll up for protection, rather as hedgehogs do. They are nocturnal, and they burrow, but do not fully hibernate. Since females have only five pairs of mammae it is likely that their litters are smaller than in the Common and Striped tenrecs.

4 Rice tenrecs *Oryzorictes*: are about 4 in (10 cm) long with a 1½ in (4 cm) flabby looking tail. Their soft fur is a dark grey-brown. The forelimbs are modified for

digging ant Rice tenrecs spend most of their time underground. like moles. They are. therefore, difficult to find although they are widely distributed in marshy areas.

5 Long-tailed tenrecs *Microgale*: furry, mousey-looking creatures with a very long tail, twice as long as the head and body. There are about 20 species, all with soft brown, grey or buff fur. They are active at all hours and occupy the same ecological niche in Madagascar as shrews do in other parts of the world.

6 Water tenrec *Limnogale*: rat-sized and very rare, these tenrecs have a very dense, soft fur like that of otters. They are semi-aquatic in habits and have a number of modifications for this way of life. They have bristle fringed forefeet and webbed hindfeet, tiny ears and a long flat tail. In contrast to other tenrecs the head is short and flat. They live beside water, feeding on invertebrates, small fish and aquatic vegetation, but little else is known about them. FAMILY: Tenrecidae, ORDER: Insectivora, CLASS: Mammalia.   P.A.M.

TENT CATERPILLARS, name given to several species of gregarious caterpillars which construct large silken webs into which they can retreat when at rest. The name is used more especially in North America, for the larvae of *Malacosoma americana* which feeds on the wild cherry and other fruit trees. Its counterpart in Europe is the Lackey moth *M. neustria*, whose larvae live gregariously in webs in their earlier stages and are also very destructive to fruit trees.

M. americana is often referred to as the Apple-tree tent caterpillar. It is the larva of a reddish-brown moth, the females of which lay their eggs in a mass around a twig early in summer. The eggs are covered with a brownish glue forming a protective layer for the nine months before they hatch. The full-grown caterpillars are about 2 in (5 cm) long, black with a white stripe down the middle of the back and with a white spot on each side of each segment of the body, which is clothed with yellowish hairs.

The eggs in a single batch may number up to 400 and the caterpillars that hatch from them combine to spin a web that takes the form of a sheet or tent stretching from one twig to another. During the day the caterpillars disperse to feed but each evening they return to the tent and huddle together in a tightly packed mass, presumably for protection. The tent is enlarged as the caterpillars grow and may ultimately be about 2 ft (60 cm) across.

It is difficult to say what benefits the caterpillars gain from this. As one writer has put it, it is not because they enjoy each other's company.

Tent caterpillars are unwelcome in orchards not only because their tents are unsightly but because they can defoliate trees. FAMILY: Lasiocampidae, ORDER: Lepidoptera, CLASS: Insecta.

TEREBELLIDS, a large family of *polychaete worms; some as large as a man's thumb, others only $\frac{2}{5} - \frac{4}{5}$ in (10–20 mm) in length, but all have numerous and highly extensible tentacles extending from the head in a medusa-like mass with which they feed. Some terebellids build tubes, others live in more or less permanent burrows in mud or within the silt which accumulates in rock crevices, merely consolidating the surrounding material with their bodies and with mucus. The Sand mason *Lanice conchilega* is perhaps an exceptionally able tube-builder. It is one of the commonest of north European terebellids and may be found, often in great abundance, in the sand or muddy sand towards low water mark. The tubes project 1 in (25 mm) or so above the surface and may be recognized by their frilly fan-shaped tops orientated towards the current. Built largely of shell-fragments and sand grains, the frilly top provides support for the tentacles which continually clean them of small particles and

A terebellid worm *Amphitrite johnstoni* removed from its burrow.

organisms on which these worms depend for food. While the tube projects from the sand, it extends vertically downwards for some distance into it and the whole tube must be carefully dug up to find the worm which rapidly descends to the bottom when alarmed.

The bodies of terebellids are commonly of moderate length and relatively muscular. The parapodia are often reduced to ridges for gripping the sides of the tube or burrow, as in so many sedentary polychaetes, and they are mostly rather helpless when removed from their homes and left on the surface of the sand, when they try to haul themselves about by means of their tentacles. One genus, *Polycirrus,* habitually does this. It lives in algal holdfasts and rock crevices and under stones, and can travel about slowly in this way, feeding on debris and small organisms as it goes. The writhing mass of usually bright orange-coloured tentacles completely conceals the remainder of the body.

Terebellids living in tubes or burrows move up and down by means of peristalsis-like movements of the body wall. This peristalsis is produced by waves of contraction and relaxation on the body wall muscles, the reduction of the septal partitions between the segments often enabling quite large and rapid movements of the fluid inside the body to occur. As the body bulges out the parapodial ridges grip the sides; as the diameter of the body is reduced in front of such a fixed point the body moves forward. When the worm is feeding the body lies near the mouth of the tube so that the tentacles can be extended from it. Peristalsis is then continued, without locomotion, in order to irrigate the tube. A flow of water is maintained over the body for respiration and to carry waste away. As with most worms respiratory exchange occurs over the whole of the body surface although terebellids have specialized gills, commonly two or three pairs, at the front end. These gills are usually quite obvious by virtue of their bright red colour due to the blood they contain.

The feeding tentacles are long and highly extensible. They are provided with ciliary gutters along which particles are conveyed to the mouth. Large particles are gripped by the sides of the tentacle and the whole tentacle pulled in. Each tentacle works more or less independently creeping forward and retracting as required, although all may be simultaneously retracted in an emergency. FAMILY: Terebellidae, CLASS: Polychaeta, PHYLUM: Annelida.   R.P.D.

TERMITES, insects closely related to cockroaches, having similar biting mouthparts and an incomplete metamorphosis. They are the most primitive insects to have developed a social system and all termites live in well regulated communities, there being no solitary forms. Approximately 2,000 species have been recognized and these are divided into six families:

Mastotermitidae, with a single living species in northern Australia representing a primitive and once widely distributed family.

Kalotermitidae, dry-wood termites.

Hodotermitidae, harvester termites in dry areas of Africa and Southeast Asia.

Termopsidae, damp-wood termites, scattered relics of an earlier age persisting in cool climates in the mountains of western USA and Asia, and in the southern tips of South America, Africa and Australasia.

Rhinotermitidae, moist-wood termites, widely distributed and destructive to timber.

Termitidae, tropical termites living in the ground or building mounds of various shapes and sizes.

Termites are polymorphic and each community is made up of several distinct castes. First in importance come the reproductives, the king and queen, or in some cases several

pairs together in one nest, Then there are the workers and soldiers and juvenile forms in various stages of development. At certain times of the year there are also present numbers of fully winged young adult termites waiting to swarm.

Winged termites vary in size according to species with wing-spans of $\frac{1}{2}-3\frac{1}{2}$ in (12–87 mm). The head is round or oval with large eyes, two small ocelli, a pair of long antennae made up of 15–32 bead-like segments and mouthparts of the biting type. Like the cockroach, the head is held at right-angles to the body. Thorax and abdomen are chitinized yellow to dark brown, and there is no narrow waist as with bees and ants. The membranous wings have a unique line of fracture close to the thorax, known as the humeral suture, which enables them to be discarded rapidly once male and female termites have found each other during swarming. The two sexes are very similar in appearance.

Worker and soldier termites are sterile individuals of either sex whose development has been arrested at an early stage. Workers have rounded heads and mandibles similar to

those of the adult. The head is chitinized but the body remains white and nymph-like. Soldiers undergo two special moults and develop large, hard heads with mandibles of a more agressive type. Only the soldiers and workers of harvester termites have functional eyes, and this is associated with their habit of feeding in daylight on plants in the open.

A large part of the community is made up of juvenile forms in various stages of growth, all white and thin skinned. Unlike bees and ants whose young are legless grubs, termites hatch out as active creatures with legs and jaws. Those which do not become workers or soldiers grow larger at each moult and gradually develop wings. These are nymphs, and at the final moult they become adult winged termites.

A queen termite develops an enlarged abdomen in order to be able to supply eggs in increasing numbers as the community grows. While the dry-wood queen only becomes a little larger, others grow a great deal and in the case of some African *Macrotermes* reach 7 in (17·5 cm) in length. Such queens are capable of producing one egg every two seconds. The king retains his original size.

Internally termites have an alimentary canal in the form of a simple tube, divided into fore-gut, mid-gut and hind-gut. The relative lengths of the last two sections depend on feeding habits. All families except the Termitidae digest their food with the aid of symbiotic Protozoa and the hind-gut is larger in order to accomodate these. Removal of these Protozoa causes the termite to die of starvation. The Termitidae rely on outside agencies such as bacteria and fungi to make wood digestible, and their mid-gut is relatively longer. The large mound building termites of tropical Africa and Asia have special fungus gardens in their nests where the food they collect is made palatable by special fungi. A number of termites feed on soil and extract nourishment from the decayed vegetation that it contains.

Termites are to be found in all the warmer regions of the world, broadly speaking between latitudes 47° north and south, but their numbers and variety are greatest in the Tropics. In Europe immigrant populations of a North American species have become established at Hamburg and near Salzburg, but the native species do not get further north than La Rochelle on the French coast, and the Crimea in southern Russia. In North

Termites or 'white ants' are social insects which have no connection with ants. Many species build the well known termite hills (up to 5 m high) from soil mixed with saliva. From the main nest innumerable tunnels, built from the same materials, run in all directions.

Opposite: soldier termite with its large jaws.

America the subterranean termite reaches the southern border of Canada, while in Japan a related species is found around Tokyo.

Tropical grasslands and deciduous woodlands support large termite populations, many kinds building large mounds to house their communities. Tropical forests also have a large variety of termites, but competition for food with other insects appears to be greater there and communities are smaller. Deserts have limited numbers of specially adapted termites which make full use of the available plant material.

The mass exodus of flying termites from the nest is known as swarming. This takes place when the weather is suitably warm and moist. Some species swarm only once or twice a year, others do so at intervals throughout the summer. All the nests of a particular species swarm together over a wide area. Day flying termites tend to congregate around trees or isolated shrubs once they are airborne, while night flying species are attracted to lights, otherwise they appear to drift along with the wind. After a short time they settle down, choosing any available area of sparse vegetation where they can scurry around in search of a mate. When this is

Winged adults, nymphs and eggs of the termite *Neotermes*.

A termitarium, housing a termite colony, rising like some bizarre ruin of a building, is built by the co-operative labours of its thousands of inhabitants.

seek out food for themselves, and soon they, in turn, feed their parents and the next batch of nymphs. These young termites turn into workers with a small proportion moulting further to become soldiers. Not until a colony has become well established over a period of years do nymphs continue their development beyond the point where they would otherwise become workers and soldiers, and with the gradual growth of wing-pads ultimately become fully grown winged termites.

Two things in particular are commonly associated with termites—their mounds and the damage they do to the woodwork of buildings. Large mounds are a feature of the tropical landscape away from the darkness of jungle or rain-forest, in the savannahs of South America, the woodlands and grassy plains of tropical Africa and the eucalyptus scrub of Australia. While superficially similar, such mounds are, in fact, built by quite different termites in each continent, in particular by *Syntermes* in South America, *Macrotermes* in Africa and southern Asia, and in Australia by *Coptotermes* and *Nasutitermes*. Small mounds come in a variety of shapes, some resemble large mushrooms, others are conical while others leave the ground altogether and are like footballs attached to the trunks and branches of trees. In Northern Australia the tall, slender, wedge-shaped mounds of *Amitermes meridionalis* always point north and south, giving it the common name of 'compass termite', and whatever advantages this may have, no other termites appear to have adopted this system. In jungles many small mounds built up against the trunks of trees have a series of steep, overhanging roofs to shed the heavy rain.

The large mounds of *Macrotermes* and *Syntermes* in the grassy plains of Africa and South America are broadly based with gently

accomplished the wings are shed and the pair move off in single file in search of shelter where they can excavate a new home. Very few of them reach this stage, however, as there are so many enemies waiting to pounce on them. Birds, lizards, ants and men are among the creatures which feed on flying termites. Those that do find a safe place proceed to dig a simple chamber, either in the ground, or in a crack at the base of a tree, or in some dead wood, and after a few days they mate and the female lays her first batch of eggs. The fragile nymphs which hatch out are fed by the parents until they are old enough to

Termites in Nigeria swarming at a lamp. Few of the insects are flying higher than the plastic-covered flex lying on the ground.

A pair of Common terns with chicks.

sloping sides and provide a foothold for trees and shrubs which cannot survive the flooding and the grass fires of the surrounding flat land. Sometimes these islands of evergreen vegetation increase in size and eventually coalesce, thus forming forest. By so doing termites influence the landscape in a way no other insect is able, returning to woodland areas cleared by man or forest fires.

Wood is the principal food of termites, and since they do not discriminate between a dead tree and timber used in buildings they have become pests of considerable economic importance. This is by no means a new problem. The kings of Ancient Egypt spent large sums of money on bringing timber from Asia Minor which was unpalatable to termites and used this for their sarcophagi. From earliest times to the present day, few accounts of travels in the Tropics are without some story of the speed with which termites have eaten items of baggage left unprotected on the ground. In villages in the desert areas of North Africa and the Middle East where much of the building is done with mud bricks, harvester termites tunnel through the walls seeking out the straw which is traditionally used in the manufacture of these bricks, and eventually the houses collapse. But termites keep pace with modern developments and they will eat the soft kinds of plastics used for insulating electric wiring or for flexible water pipes. In Northern Australia there is a particularly voracious termite which attacks the lead covering of underground telephone cables.

Less well known is the value of termites as food for other animals, including man. Flying termites are well supplied with fat and proteins in order that they may start new colonies without having to leave the shelter of their chamber to forage for food. Thus they are attractive to a large variety of animals, especially when swarming takes place at the beginning of the wet season before other food sources have recovered from the effects of the dry summer. Birds in particular are active when swarming termites appear, and some migrant species in Africa appear to time their movements to coincide with local swarming periods. Social wasps in South America provision their huge nests with large numbers of winged termites, choosing just those kinds whose size best fits the individual cells. Men collect termites for food in many lands, and they are to be found in village markets offered for sale, particularly in countries where meat is scarce. The large, sausage-shaped queen from large mounds in Africa and Asia are regarded as delicacies. Chimpanzees in tropical Africa eat soldier termites which they collect by poking sticks down the holes leading to the nests of various species. The alarmed soldiers grasp the intruding stick in their powerful jaws hang on when the stick is withdrawn, to be scraped off by the chimpanzee and chewed up. ORDER: Isoptera, CLASS: Insecta, PHYLUM: Arthropoda.   W.V.H.

TERMITE WEEDKILLERS. Termites of the family Termitidae rely on bacteria and fungi to make wood digestible. One species, *Odontotermes redemanni,* cultivates only one species of fungus in its 'gardens'. It has been found that if the termites are kept out of the 'garden' other fungi invade it, so the termites are actively cultivating a crop. They do this by means of a chemical weedkiller, caprylic acid. The acid is secreted from the anus of the queen termite and licked up by the workers who then transfer it to the 'garden' when cementing particles of 'soil' together. Its effect is to prevent spores of other fungi from germinating.

TERNS, constitute the subfamily Sterninae, of the family Laridae, which includes about 43 species of birds that resemble gulls, but are mostly smaller and more lightly built, often with long forked tails. They are short-legged birds with webbed feet and a bill that is long and tapers to a point in all but one species. They all have long, pointed wings and most have deeply forked tails, hence the old name of 'Sea swallows'. Most species are white with a grey back and wings and a black cap on the head in the breeding season, though this is often lost in the winter. Some have black upperparts in the breeding season, a few species also having a black breast.

Most terns (37 species) are classified in the genus *Sterna*. These can be divided into several groups, the typical black-capped species being the most numerous. In Britain the Common tern *Sterna hirundo,* the Arctic tern *S. paradisaea* and the Roseate tern *S. dougallii* are representatives of this group. They are mainly coastal birds that feed on small fishes caught by plunging into the water from a height. The Arctic tern is remarkable in that it probably enjoys more hours of daylight each year than any other bird. It breeds as far north as about 82°N and migrates south in the autumn to winter in Antarctic and subantarctic waters. This group also includes a freshwater species, the smaller Black-bellied tern *S. melanogaster* of southern Asia. The crested tern group has several species of medium to large size. The Sandwich tern *S. sandvicensis* is the only species to breed in Britain; it migrates to South Africa and the surrounding seas for the winter. The largest of all the terns, the Caspian tern *S. tschegrava,* belongs in this group, it is about the size of a Herring gull and breeds in scattered places in Europe, Africa, Asia, North America, Australia and New Zealand. Other rather smaller crested species are the Crested or Swift tern *S. bergii,* the Elegant tern *S. elegans* and the Royal tern *S. maxima.*

Then there is a small group of little terns, the most common of which is the widely distributed Little or Least tern *S. albifrons.* This is a small species with a black cap in breeding plumage, the forehead remaining white throughout the year. The Marsh tern group differs from the others (except the Gull-billed tern *S. nilotica*) in being much less closely tied to water. Included in this group are the Black tern *S. nigra,* the White-winged black tern *S. leucopterus* and the Whiskered tern *S. hybrida.* Like the other members of this genus they are colonial nesters, but they breed on the reed-fringed shores of lakes and rivers, in freshwater marshes and on swampy grasslands. The Black tern breeds in Europe, Asia and in the middle latitudes of North America, but the other two species are confined to Europe and Asia. Rather separate from the others of the genus, are the Large-billed tern *S. simplex* and the Gull-billed tern *S. nilotica.* The latter has an almost cosmopolitan distribution and feeds by catching large insects, lizards, small frogs and other animals found in the grassland, and sometimes by picking small animals from the surface of freshwater or estuaries.

Opposite, top: the greatest wanderer on earth, the Arctic tern migrates from Arctic to Antarctic and back again, a distance of 22,000 miles (36,000 km) a year.

Opposite, bottom: Noddy terns on the island of Aldabra in the Indian Ocean.

The genus *Anous* includes five species called noddies that frequent tropical seas. These are described in a separate entry.

Most terns have harsh calls, though many species have a considerable vocabulary: long drawn out wavering notes, short yapping calls and repeated screeches. Courtship feeding with fishes, attractive hovering display flights and imitation nest-making figure prominently in their courtship behaviour.

Terns are very social birds and often breed in large colonies. The *Sterna* species nest either in bare scrapes in the ground, or in flimsy nests made from seaweed and other local materials. The Common noddy lays its egg on bare rock, in a nest of seaweed and twigs on the ground, or in a nest built in bushes or even low trees. Noddies lay only a single egg in each clutch, but the *Sterna* species lay clutches of two or three eggs; the eggs are usually grey or brown in colour with dark brown and pale grey-brown spots and blotches. Incubation periods vary from about 19 to 26 days and both sexes sit. The chicks are active and alert within a few hours of hatching and are covered with thick down that is cryptically marked in most species. Fledging periods vary from about four to eight weeks. The noddies that nest in trees start to fly from the moment they leave the nest, but the *Sterna* species begin to wander away from the nest soon after hatching and only then start gradually to fly.

Most terns feed mainly on fishes that they catch by plunge-diving into the sea from some height, but the Marsh terns pick food from the surface of water and hawk insects in the air. The Gull-billed tern hawks insects and also catches insects and other small animals on the surface of grassland.

Most of the terns breeding in northern areas migrate southwards for the winter, the Arctic tern migrating from the Arctic to the Antarctic, taking advantage of both summers. The tropical species do not migrate, or at least they do not move far. Recent research has shown that the Sooty tern *S. fuscata* breeds in nine and a half month cycles in the tropical Atlantic. These cycles may correspond to cycles in the abundance of the fishes on which they feed in these essentially unseasonal latitudes. FAMILY: Laridae, ORDER: Charadriiformes, CLASS: Aves.   D.H.

TERRAPINS, name given to the seven geographical races of *Malaclemys terrapin* living in the eastern part of North America. They are moderate-sized turtles with a carapace up to about 10 in (25 cm) long. The individual scutes of the dorsal carapace are often in the shape of a truncated cone and clearly concentrically grooved, so that in America they are called 'Diamondback terrapins'. They live in the sea and in salt and brackish water lakes along the Atlantic coast

In spite of its name, *Terrapene carolina*, this is the Eastern box turtle, not one of the species normally referred to as a terrapin.

of North America, from Massachusetts southward to the Yucatan Peninsula in Mexico, and the Florida keys. Like many seabirds and like marine turtles, terrapins have special glands behind the corner of the eye to secrete the excess salt from the body. Nevertheless, salt seems to be vital to them, since if they are kept for a long time in fresh-water only, they develop ulcers, no longer eat and finally die.

Terrapins usually stay in the water, but are also said to travel considerable distances on land, if they cannot find a promising place to lay their eggs. They live chiefly on small crustaceans and molluscs, but also take a small amount of vegetable food.

Terrapins are highly esteemed delicacies. At one time they were sold on the markets and formed an everyday item of food. In the 18th century there was even a rising of the slaves, who were protesting that they were too often given the fat flesh of these turtles. Owing to the excessive persecution by human beings and the cultivation of the coastal areas the terrapin population has been so drastically

reduced, however, that they are now being bred in terrapin farms. They cost about seven dollars each.

In Britain almost any small freshwater turtle of any kind is likely to be called a terrapin. In the United States many people use the word for any edible freshwater turtle. Strictly speaking it should be reserved for one species only, *Malaclemys terrapin*. See turtles. FAMILY: Emyidae, ORDER: Testudines, CLASS: Reptilia. J.H.M.

TERRITORY, an area defended by an animal against other members of its species. It was the English ornithologist, Eliot Howard, who first outlined the main principles of this important factor in the behaviour of many animals in the wild. He saw that with the coming of spring the winter flocks of Reed warblers began to break up, each male seeking out an area of reeds where it perched and sang; at intervals they would return to the flock. But as the season went on their desertions of the territory grew less and each became aggressive towards other Reed

warblers. Boundary fights with neighbours established the confines of the territories into which females were lured. After pair formation the female also learned the boundaries and helped in their defence. Mating and nesting took place in the territory.

Although many birds mark out a territory around a nest, this is not essential. Wheatears, for example, will defend a territory before nest-building. At this stage both male and female combine to drive off other wheatears, but their reactions are stronger when the nest is built and all birds whatever their species are then driven away.

Among birds there are various sizes and functions of territory. It may serve both as a nesting, mating and feeding area. This is typical of many songbirds which spend much of their time on their own territories only leaving them for any period to go to an area not already occupied by a bird of their own species. Amongst European passerines territories range in area from 1,200–2,400 sq yd (1,000–2,000 sq m) to 2½ acres (1 ha). The territory may only be for mating and

which serves only as a nesting place. Thus Herring gulls do not mate or feed on their territory, which may nevertheless be quite a large area around the nest, although if the population is large, the individual territories will be very much smaller. Sometimes, with colonial nesters, like the Guira cuckoo, all the females band together to protect the area. House sparrows and finches have territories which, like those of the gulls, are limited to the nest.

When male birds of the same species meet at their territorial frontiers they perform *agonistic displays which are threats directed at the opponent. Usually such displays suffice to cause one or other to retreat. If one bird leaves his territory and happens to enter that of the other, his aggressiveness declines sharply and he retreats. His opponent follows, entering the defeated bird's territory, then the roles are reversed and the contest moves back. This oscillation to-and-fro may go on for a little time before one bird gives up and flies away. The same aggressiveness is shown to a female but because she takes up a submissive posture the male's desire to attack is reduced and the female can enter his territory, but once the pair-bond is established no other female will be admitted.

Similar sorts of behaviour can be seen in fishes, a number of which are territorial. Thus, the male Three-spined stickleback makes a nest of filamentous algae, glueing the structure with secretions from his kidneys. He then defends the area around the nest, threatening intruding fishes by turning nose-down and erecting his dorsal and ventral spines. The place at which such a display will take place is determined by the combats between neighbours, just as the boundaries of a bird's territory are demarcated. Territorial boundaries are not necessarily marked by natural objects so that, although the bounds are quite clear to the fish it may be extremely difficult for a human being to see them. Cichlid fishes also defend a territory, and two males will fight by using their tails to beat water at their opponents. They first swim in a circle nose to tail, threatening each other by expanding their throat regions beneath their gill-covers and spreading their fins. The more aggressive fish butts its rival and when one gives in to prevent further attack it signals this, by adopting a submissive attitude in which the fins are lowered and the gill-covers closed to the body. A male bitterling will defend a territory around the freshwater mussel which it has chosen as the one in which it will induce a female to lay eggs.

Insects too will defend a territory, thus a male dragonfly will have a particular promenading place on a river bank from which it will drive off other males.

Many mammals have a small area which they defend but a much bigger area, the home range, over which they move with comparative ease to feed and into which others wander with impunity. A chipmunk, for example, has a territory of about 50 yd (45 m) radius, but a home range of twice that size. Often the size of the territory seems to be correlated with food-gathering, each animal occupying an area large enough for it to gain sufficient food for itself. On the plains of Africa the size of the territory of a carnivore is often much larger than that of a herbivore. Whereas the grass-eating animal can find abundant food within a small area, a carnivore has to hunt more widely to find its prey. Thus, in the Albert National Park, a lion's territory was $1-1\frac{1}{2}$ sq miles (3 or 4 sq km) but there were three hippopotamuses to $\frac{1}{3}$ sq mile (1 sq km) or 12 Topi antelopes, 24 Kob antelopes and two reedbucks to $\frac{1}{3}$ sq mile (1 sq km). A lion would not permit another lion to enter its territory but would allow hyaenas to come in.

The territory and home range of an ungulate in the wild is a network of well-trodden paths connecting feeding places, bathing places, excreting and drinking places with a protected area around the 'home'. All these trails are firmly fixed and one might say that familiarity with its territory is a 'comfort' to such an animal. Herbivorous animals do not usually feed around their home and the long grass that is left serves as cover. It is quite common for animals not to eat in the immediate neighbourhood of their main home. Anteaters, for example, may even burrow into termite nests by their home but leave the insects unharmed though they feed on termites in other nests, and carnivores, both birds and mammals, often seem to kill their prey only at places beyond a certain distance from their home or nest.

Mammal territories may also be held by a group rather than a breeding pair. The dominant male woodmouse marks out a territory of 4–6 acres ($1\frac{1}{2}-2\frac{1}{2}$ ha) which is used by the whole colony. It is regularly patrolled to keep out intruders. Howler monkeys move about in clans consisting of, for example, three adult males, eight females, three dependant infants and four juveniles. They range through the trees over an area which forms the clan's territory. Any rival clan intruding into the territory is greeted with a barking roar, low-pitched and sonorous, made by the males; the noise is then so great that the forest reverberates. At dawn the cries of the Howlers re-establishing their territories are among the most striking features of the forest life in Panama. Prairie dog towns consist of areas which are the territories of coteries within it, defended against others. The young of any of the groups are permitted to wander through the defended areas but there is a gradual increase in the adult's aggressive response to the young as they grow. In this way, they come to learn

nesting. This is the case for many of the colonial nesting seabirds like gannets, the densely packed colonies of which contain nests which, with a very small area around them, are defended aggressively by their owners. The birds fly off to sea to feed and mix together while doing so. A territory may be for mating only. Gould's manakin is an example. The male bird clears a 'court', an area about 20×30 in (50×75 cm) from which he removes every leaf or twig leaving bare earth. He stays in the vicinity during the daylight hours and drives off other males. When he sees a female of his own species he begins an elaborate display to attract her. If she succumbs to this, she enters the arena and the two perform a mutual leaping 'dance' after which they fly off elsewhere to mate and nest. Some territories are for feeding alone; such areas are often held outside the breeding season. The winter territory of the robin is an example. It is defended by both male and female, while that of the blackbird is defended by the females alone. Finally, there is the territory the boundaries of their own coterie's area.

So widespread among animals is territorial behaviour that one feels it must have profound significance, but it is not at all easy to do more than conjecture about its function. First, no doubt, it tends to distribute animals so that an area can take maximum numbers. By preventing clumping together it spreads them out so that they make more effective use of the ground. This enforced distribution may have another effect if the animals are cryptically coloured as are some birds and their eggs, for it may maximize the effectiveness of this camouflage. Should the birds be close together, if a predator finds one it finds all of them but spaced out each is as difficult as the next one to locate. A second advantage may be that of preventing overcrowding. As the population density goes up, the territories become more squeezed together and reduced in size, but this increases the aggressiveness of the territory owners until territories reach an irreducible minimum size. Then birds must seek territories on the borders of the area until then occupied by the population and in this way an increase of the breeding range may be brought about as the birds are pushed farther out.

There are also special advantages in reproduction derived from the existence of territories. Much *courtship consists of mutual behaviour between male and female which has the effect of bringing them fully and finally into the physiological state which is necessary for successful mating. The defence of a territory keeps the pair together and at an earlier stage ensures that the male is fixed to one area and is therefore easier for the female to locate. Communal display grounds of birds, like ruffs, are effective because of the attractiveness to the females of a group of male birds behaving conspicuously. The females, having arrived, will each leave with one of the males. But territory has its fourth advantage in being a quiet spot where the gradual and delicate process of courtship can go on uninterrupted. Once the physiological changes are initiated it is important that they continue undisturbed until their culmination.

Success in marking out territory is of the utmost importance to some species. The breeding success of grouse, for example, depends very much on the size of territory which has been seized by the male. Each autumn there is a contest between males for the available areas of heather. These end in a number of territories being marked. Subsequently, the unsuccessful birds, which may be as many as 50% of the population, are nearly all killed by predators, succumb to disease or die in other ways. On the other hand very few of the pairs, hen and cock, on the territories die. When the pressure on space is less, because the population is de-

clining, the males take larger territories. And the more vigorous a male (and the more aggressive) the bigger will be its territory. But the size of territory bears no relation, in this case, to the amount of food available within it. Survival of the chicks depends largely upon the nutrition of their parents in the previous year, not on what can now be obtained in the territory.

It might seem that territory in birds has the function of rationing out the environment in terms of the food it contains. On the whole, although birds of the same species are not allowed to enter another's territory, other

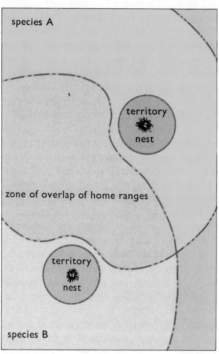

Comparison of home range and territory in an animal's normal living area. Parts of a home range may normally be occupied by two or more members of a species, whereas a territory is normally defended against others of the same species.

species are permitted to move in and out freely. Indeed, territories of different species will often overlap. In general, two species occupying the same geographical area are not feeding upon exactly the same food and, therefore, they are not competing with each other for the available food supplies. Other members of the same species, however, will be doing so, and their exclusion means that the food is reserved to the pair occupying the territory. The food requirements of a pair which is feeding nestlings are very great and where food is not over-abundant, territory may serve as a means of apportioning the food supply. Where territories are not used for feeding it is usually because there is ample food for all, as there is, more especially, in the sea. Territories for feeding lose their importance and, in fact, many colonial nesting seabirds have territories confined to the nest. Those of mammals seem to be

much more a matter of control of food supply than those of birds. In *Apodemus sylvaticus* population numbers are kept steady because the dominant males drive off the young, forcing them to keep out of the way or to disperse. The result of this intraspecific control is that the populations of this mouse do not undergo the violent fluctuations that are seen in many other small mammals, e.g. shrews.

Ownership of a territory is indicated in many ways. The familiar sound of bird song is often the territorial call of the male, perhaps the most characteristic song of most species. Among songbirds, this kind of song is given from a prominent song-post in the territory and warns other males away, while at the same time attracting females—at least at the beginning of the breeding season. The cries of Prairie dogs and of Howler monkeys are other examples of territorial defence calls. Visual displays are also used by territory owners, as, for example, the signals of Fiddler crabs. Its claw-waving is effective in keeping away other males from its burrows. Scent marks are used by many mammals. Various ungulates have facial glands the secretion of which is wiped on bushes or twigs to indicate ownership of the area. Red deer will mark their territories in this way. Other ungulates like the muntjac have glands on their feet which deposit scented material on the ground. But it is not always glandular secretions which are used. Dogs which urinate on lamp-posts are marking their territory. A lion will urinate on the ground and then rub its feet in the urine, thus its tracks will be marked with the odour. Pine martens use faeces at points in their territory. Hippopotamuses live mainly in rivers but they have territories on the land beside the river, each of them fanning out over the countryside. These areas are covered by well-used trails which are marked at intervals by their owners. The odoriforous material is a mixture of urine and faeces which is scattered by a rapidly wagging tail. Many mammals sharpen their claws and when doing this frequently transfer scent to the tree. A Wild cat, for example, will urinate and, having put its paws in the urine will, afterwards, claw a post leaving the scent on the bark. The Water vole, *Arvicola*, makes use of secretions from flank glands which are transferred to the hindfeet and then stamped onto the ground.

Territorial behaviour is often restricted to the breeding season. This is particularly so in birds who in the winter come together to form flocks of both sexes. But even in a group of birds like this, there is still what may be considered as the vestiges of territory. When two of them get too close together, one will threaten and drive the other away. There is an individual distance within which another bird will be attacked. It is as if each bird now had a small territory around itself. This is not true of all birds, for some are contact species and they tend to huddle together as closely as possible. But in the distant species maintenance of individual distance seems to be of the utmost importance.   J.D.C.

TESTACEANS, free-living amoeboid protozoans; the body protoplasm is contained within a single-chambered shell or test. See amoebae, testate.

TESTUDINES, a reptilian order which includes all tortoises, turtles, and terrapins and belongs to the subclass Anapsida. The most obvious feature is the exoskeleton enclosing the body and which is composed of the dorsal carapace and ventral plastron. Typically the exoskeleton consists of an inner bony layer covered by an external layer of horn. The exoskeleton may be much reduced in aquatic types. The trunk vertebrae are reduced in number and together with the ribs become incorporated in the carapace. The jaws of all species, fossil and living, are toothless being covered by horny plates which macerate plant food or soft animal foods.

The oldest known is the Triassic genus *Proganochelys*. This and other primitive chelonians were incapable of retracting the head within the box-like exoskeleton. Two more advanced groups which can retract the head are recognised: the Cryptodira and Pleurodira. CLASS: Reptilia.

TETHYS SEA or Tethys Ocean, the sea which partially separated the supercontinents of Laurasia and Gondwanaland before these were split up by *continental drift. Its eastern half was obliterated by the movement of India and Arabia into Asia, but its western half remains, though narrowed, as the Mediterranean.

TETRAHYMENA, a small ciliate protozoan, of which about 12 species are known. *Tetrahymena* has been intensively studied because it represents a primitive ciliate and also because the ease with which it can be maintained in the laboratory has made it a well-used model for cell biologists and physiologists. It is egg-shaped when viewed from the side and the mouth is not at the front end, as is usual in ciliates, but is situated slightly to one side towards the anterior and narrower pole. The covering of cilia is uniform and the mouth bears a number of fused cilia in a characteristic arrangement consisting of three groups fused to the left and a row fused to produce an undulating membrane to the right. The macronucleus is round or almost round. Some of the species of *Tetrahymena* are completely free-living, others are facultative parasites, that is, they are normally free-living but become parasitic

if the chance occurs. Others are parasitic but can become free-living and others are parasites all their lives. The normal method of reproduction is by asexual division, but the sexual process of conjugation does occur as it does in most ciliates. Cysts are not formed by *Tetrahymena*, which is therefore confined to permanently moist habitats. ORDER: Hymenostomatida, CLASS: Ciliata, PHYLUM: Protozoa.   F.E.G.C.

TETRAPODA, literally four-footed beasts, is the Greek-derived equivalent of the more commonly used 'quadruped'. Tetrapods include Amphibia, Reptilia and Mammalia, but fishes are sometimes included.

THALIACEA, a class of planktonic marine *Sea squirts in which the primitive ability to reproduce asexually by budding has been developed to provide life-histories of sometimes extraordinary complication. In general, individuals hatched from an egg do not possess the ability to reproduce sexually, only by budding, forming long chains of individuals. In the most complex form of life-history these primary budded individuals then bud again to produce another chain of different form and these alone are capable of sexual reproduction. Like all Sea squirts Thaliacea feed by filtering seawater, but do so by swimming along engulfing water at the mouth and passing it out via the gills and the 'atrial siphon'. See also *Salpa, Doliolum, Pyrosoma.* SUBPHYLUM Urochordata, PHYLUM: Chordata.

THAMIN *Cervus eldi,* a swamp dwelling *deer of Southeast Asia, also known as Eld's deer or the Brow-antlered deer.

THECODONTS, extinct reptiles that lived about 200 million years ago and which probably represent the ancestral stock from which dinosaurs, pterodactyls, crocodiles and birds were derived. They were generally small, a few feet (1 m) long and they received their name because their teeth were implanted in deep sockets, each tooth being hollow at the base with its successor developing in that hollow. Most of them were terrestrial but some lived in shallow water and many of them showed a tendency to become bipedal. Most of them were probably herbivores but there were some at least which were definitely flesh-eaters and these were larger than usual with very large skulls. ORDER: Thecodontia, SUBCLASS: Archosauria, CLASS: Reptilia.

THERAPSIDA, extinct reptiles that lived during the Permian and Triassic period 270–180 million years ago. Their remains have been found mainly in South Africa, but others have been collected from America, Europe and Asia. They ranged in size from that of a rat to massive beasts 13 ft (4 m) long

and they are important because their skulls show some of the features of mammalian skulls, especially in the bony arch between the orbit and the openings to the rear of the skull. ORDER: Therapsida, SUBCLASS: Synapsida, CLASS: Reptilia.

THERIA, a subclass of the class Mammalia which includes the infraclass Metatheria or *marsupials and the infraclass Eutheria or true or placental *mammals.

THEROPODA, a suborder of carnivorous *dinosaurs 10–50 ft (3·0–15 m) long, with long, strong hindlegs, small front legs and long powerful tail used no doubt as a balancer when the reptile was running bipedally. The teeth, set in sockets in the jaws, were sabre-like, often with serrated edges. One of the best known theropods is *Tyrannosaurus.* ORDER: Saurischia, SUBCLASS: Synapsida, CLASS: Reptilia.

THICKHEADS, the subfamily Pachycephalinae of Oriental-Australasian flycatchers, also called whistlers from their loud melodious songs. They vary from the size of a finch to that of a jay. They have largish heads and often heavy bills, and feed mainly on insects and invertebrates. They build open, cup-shaped nests. The plumage is frequently green and yellow, sometimes rufous and grey; and the head often has a conspicuous black and white pattern. Some species have crests. They take food from the ground or from plants rather than from the air. In Australia some species are called robins and fill a similar role around farms and houses to the European robin. FAMILY: Muscicapidae, ORDER: Passeriformes, CLASS: Aves.

THICK-KNEES, a family of plover-like birds of which the species are variously, and sometimes alternatively, known by this name and by others such as Stone curlew and (from Afrikaans) dikkop. The characteristic thickening of the leg is at the intertarsal joint, which is often mistakenly thought to be the knee. There is no affinity with the curlews proper, nor any resemblance in the shape of the bill. For details see Stone curlew. FAMILY: Burhinidae, ORDER: Charadriiformes, CLASS: Aves.

THIRD EYELID, or *nictitating membrane, a membrane under the other two eyelids that can be drawn across the eyeball.

THIRST SNAKES, so called because one of their genera is named *Dipsas,* after a serpent of Greek legend whose bite caused a raging thirst, are small inoffensive snakes that feed solely on slugs and snails. Nocturnal and mostly arboreal, Thirst snakes have long needle-like teeth enabling the snake to grip the soft slimy prey, and they lack the chin groove,

The Thirst snake *Dipsas turgidus* seen here feeding on a snail.

a characteristic feature of snakes which makes a wide stretching of the jaws possible. Those Thirst snakes that eat snails are expert at withdrawing the mollusc from its shell.

There are 16 species of Thirst snake in Southeast Asia, nearly all in the genus *Pareas,* and others in Central and South America, including *Dipsas,* which eats snails, and *Sibon,* which appears to eat only slugs. FAMILY: Colubridae, ORDER: Squamata, CLASS: Reptilia.

THOMPSON, D'A, W., 1860–1948, British biologist, classical scholar and mathematician. Educated in science at Cambridge, and with a strong classical background, D'Arcy Thompson was an outstanding counter-influence to the separation of 'the two cultures'. President of the Classical Associations of England and Wales and of Scotland; Professor of Natural History at University College, Dundee, later the University of St Andrews, for a total of 64 years; and distinguished in mathematics, he was elected Fellow of the Royal Society in 1916 and was Vice-President from 1931–1933. He was knighted in 1937.

D'Arcy Thompson's scientific publications range widely over much of zoology, with emphasis on aquatic animals. For over 50 years he was involved in various national and international fisheries projects. His books include *A Glossary of Greek Birds* (1895), *Science and the Classics* (1940), and *A Glossary of Greek Fishes* (1947), but by far his most important work, was *On Growth and Form,* first published in 1917. In

this work, written in exquisite style, he expresses various aspects of the structure and development of animals in mathematical and physical terms, showing that, mathematically-speaking 'whatsoever is most beautiful and regular is also found to be most useful and excellent'.

THORNBACK RAY, a common species of ray in which the spines on the back and pectoral fins are very well developed. See also rays.

THORNY-HEADED WORMS, parasitic worms, the adults of which grow and reproduce in the intestines of vertebrates (final hosts) and the developmental stages of which are found in the body cavities of arthropods, including insects and crustaceans (intermediate hosts). The final host becomes infected by eating an intermediate host containing the parasite.

The earliest reports of Acanthocephala, the scientific name for Thorny-headed worms, were made independently by the Italian, Francesco Redi and Anton van Leeuwenhoek of Holland, towards the end of the 17th century and, since then, about 650 species have been described. 21 families of Acanthocephala are recognized and three classes, Archiacanthocephala, Paleacanthocephala and Eoacanthocephala. Not all biologists treat Acanthocephala as a phylum, the approach adopted here, but view it rather as a class within the phylum Aschelminthes. Mature worms of the majority of species of Acanthocephala are about $\frac{1}{2}$–1 in ($1\frac{1}{4}$–$2\frac{1}{2}$

cm) long. Female worms are longer than males and the longest acanthocephalan discovered to date is the female *Nephridiacanthus longissimus* from the intestine of aardvarks. This worm is about 37 in (93 cm) long. Most acanthocephalans are white, but some, like *Polymorphus minutus* from ducks, are bright orange owing to carotenoid pigments taken in with their food and dissolved in the fat in the parasite's body wall.

The diagnostic character of the group is the hook-bearing, retractile proboscis by means of which they become attached to their host's intestinal wall. The proboscis is everted by a hydraulic system and is withdrawn by muscular contraction into the proboscis sheath; the everting fluid then flows into the two lemnisci which are organs characteristic of Acanthocephala. The proboscis and associated tissues are called the praesoma, while the rest of the body is called the metasoma.

The female reproductive system consists of an ovary, uterine bell, muscular uterus and vagina. When the female is mature, the ovary disintegrates to release ovarian balls into the body cavity. After these have been fertilized they break up to reveal the developing eggs. The eggs develop in the female's body cavity and those which have reached the full larval stage, known as an acanthor, and are therefore infective to the intermediate host are selected by the uterine bell and discharged from the worm. Immature larvae remain in the body cavity for further development.

The body wall of an acanthocephalan worm has skeletal, protective, absorptive and metabolic functions. The fibres of the radial and felt layers and the stabilized protein cuticle provide the skeletal function and protection from mechanical damage while an epicuticle of mucopolysaccharide may help to protect the worm from the host's digestive enzymes. The absorption of nutrients occurs through the numerous tiny pores which penetrate the cuticle. Acanthocephalans never possess an alimentary tract at any stage of their life-history. Metabolic functions can be assigned to the body wall because it contains much stored glycogen and lipid and many *mitochondria. The mitochondria have small cristae, indicating that the adult worms obtain their energy independently of oxygen. Very few species of Acanthocephala have excretory organs and the body wall is probably involved in the excretion of waste products.

Once the mature eggs, each of them containing an acanthor larva, have been discharged from the final host in its faeces, they must be eaten by the correct intermediate host before development can continue: insects for those which reproduce in terrestrial vertebrates and usually crustaceans for those which infect aquatic final hosts. The mature egg consists of an acanthor larva enclosed in four egg shells. When this has been eaten by an appropriate intermediate host, the acanthor escapes from the shells in the host's mid-gut and either bores into the intestinal wall or into the body cavity beyond. The acanthor gradually changes to an acanthella larva which grows rapidly and is always found free in the host's body cavity. When development in the intermediate host has been completed, the acanthella goes into a resting stage known as the cystacanth which is not activated until the intermediate host is eaten by the correct final host.

On reaching the intestine of the final host, the proboscis of the cystacanth is everted and the parasite becomes established in the region of the final host's intestine which forms the environment of the adult worm. Sometimes an intermediate host containing a cystacanth is eaten by a vertebrate which acts as a transport host rather than a final host capable of supporting mature worms. After being activated in the transport host's intestine, the cystacanth migrates into that host's abdominal tissues where it re-encysts and becomes dormant again until the transport host is eaten by a suitable final host. Transport hosts are important in ensuring that acanthocephalan parasites of large vertebrate predators, like seals and carnivorous fishes, which rarely eat arthropods, become established in their final hosts. PHYLUM: Acanthocephala.

D.W.T.C.

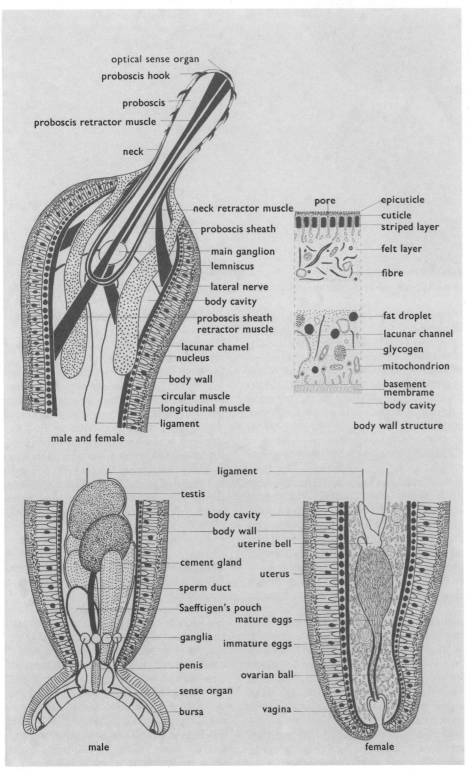

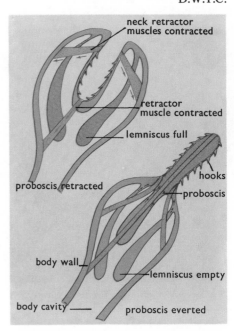

Above: the mechanism of everting the proboscis in Thorny-headed worms.

Left: anatomy of a Thorny-headed worm.

THRASHERS, medium sized thrush-like birds, 9–13 in (23–33 cm) long, brown or grey-brown above and white below. The bill is long or moderately long and is often highly curved. There are large, black spots on the breast in some species but these are faint or absent in others. Thrashers are found mainly in the arid southwest of the United States and northern Mexico and on certain Caribbean islands. Two species breed in southern Canada, the Brown thrasher *Toxostoma rufum* in the east and the Sage thrasher *Oreoscoptes montanus* in the west.

The thrashers are at best a poorly defined subgroup of the mockingbird family Mimidae and may or may not represent a single line of evolution. Four distinct groups, based on the nature of the spotting on the breast feathers, are recognizable in the major thrasher genus *Toxostoma*. Least typical of the thrashers is the Sage thrasher which behaves more like a mockingbird *Mimus polyglottos* except on the ground where it runs and digs like a typical *Toxostoma* thrasher. Also unusual is the trembler, *Cinclocerthia ruficauda* of the West Indies, whose whole body continually shivers.

The Curve-billed thrasher *Toxostoma curvirostra* lives in the desert brush of the southwestern United States and northern Mexico.

Typical thrashers feed on a wide variety of insects, wild fruits and seeds which they normally take from the ground. Leaf litter and soil is turned over using the bill which has become adapted in a number of species for use as a pick. This specialization probably arose from the use of the bill as a hammer, which is seen in such non-specialized forms as the Brown thrasher when it tackles harder seeds and nuts. The Curve-billed thrasher *Toxostoma curvirostra* has been seen to excavate holes up to $2\frac{1}{2}$ in (6 cm) deep in its search for grubs.

During the breeding season thrashers are territorial and the males sing a generally musical, warbling song with occasional mimicry of the songs of other birds. The nest is built low down in a thick bush or even on the ground and normally in an impenetrable situation. It is well defended, the adults of some species attacking even human intruders. It is made from concentric baskets of progressively finer materials: twigs, leaves, grasses and finally fine material. It holds a clutch of 3–6 eggs, pale bluish or whitish with dark brown or reddish markings. Incubation and fledging both take about 12 days and a second brood is started in a new nest immediately the first is on the wing.

Thrashers are mainly ground dwelling birds which seldom fly. Some prefer to run when disturbed. They live in thick scrub or dense shrubberies with plenty of bare soil or leaf litter. Where two species with similar requirements share the same geographical range they show distinct habitat preferences. Thus the California thrasher *Toxostoma redivivum* inhabits the dense cover of the chaparral in the area where the Crissal thrasher *T. dorsale* lives in the mesquite. FAMILY: Mimidae, ORDER: Passeriformes, CLASS: Aves.   J.H.M.

THREAD-FINS, perch-like fishes distantly related to the barracudas and the Grey mullets. They are marine and estuarine fishes found in all tropical waters. Their name derives from the form of the pectoral fin, which is in two distinct parts. The upper part bears the normal complement of branching rays but the lower part is made up of about six long filamentous rays unconnected by a membrane. The elongated rays can be moved independently of each other and it is thought that they may have some sensory function, possibly serving as organs of touch since these fishes inhabit murky waters.

Thread-fins have compressed bodies with the spiny first dorsal fin and the soft-rayed second dorsal fin well separated, as found in the barracudas and Grey mullets. The snout is pointed and overhangs the mouth, as in many fishes that grub on the bottom.

Thread-fins are valuable fishes since they are not only good to eat but provide a type of isinglass from their swimbladders. The largest species is *Eleutheronema tetradactylum* (i.e. four-fingers) from the Indian Ocean. It is sometimes called the Burnett salmon and off the coasts of India it has been known to reach 6 ft (1·8 m) and to weigh up to 320 lb (145 kg). Because of its rather pinkish flesh it has been given the name 'salmon'. The fish is a pale blue-grey with a yellow eye and yellow on the upper part of the pectoral fin. Blue and yellow are common colours in the thread-fins. *Polynemus sheridani,* a smaller species which reaches 18 in (45 cm) in length, has yellow on the lower half of the body, while the Striped thread-fin *P. plebejus* has a bluish body with fine yellow horizontal stripes. FAMILY: Polynemidae, ORDER: Perciformes, CLASS: Pisces.

THREAD SNAKES, superficially similar to *Blind snakes, are burrowers, small and wormlike, 6–10 in (15–25 cm) in length, with only vestiges of a pelvis and hindlimbs. Lower jaw teeth are numerous, but the upper jaw, which is immoveably fixed to the rest of the skull, has no teeth. The eyes are hidden beneath head scales. Thread snakes, of which there is only one genus, *Leptotyphlops*, are found in Africa, southwest Asia, and also in the New World, in savannahs and semi-desert regions. A few elongated eggs are laid. The food of Thread snakes consists largely of termites. FAMILY: Leptotyphlopidae, ORDER: Squamata, CLASS: Reptilia.

THREAD WORM, one of the common names used for members of the Nematoda, many of which are slender and thread-like in appearance. The name *'roundworm' is, however, more frequently employed to designate this group of invertebrates.

THRESHER SHARKS, *Alopias vulpinus* and two very similar species, large shark-like fishes characterized by the enormous upper lobe of the tail, which may be equal to the length of the rest of the body. The Thresher sharks have a world-wide distribution in tropical and temperate seas, mainly living a pelagic life in the upper waters but with at least one species found in deep water. In general form they resemble the Grey sharks but their enormous tail easily identifies them. Stories of threshers using their tails to lash at whales, while swordfishes execute a *coup de grâce* with their swords, are quite without foundation, but there are reliable accounts of the thresher using its tail to stun or kill fishes and birds at the surface, which it then eats. There is still some doubt, however, whether threshers really encircle shoals of fishes and with their tails beat them into a compact mass before charging in and feasting. The threshers reach about 20 ft (6 m) in length and may weigh up to 1,000 lb (454 kg). The young are hatched within the uterus of the female and when born are 4½–5 ft (1·2–1·5 m) long. FAMILY: Alopiidae, ORDER: Pleurotremata, CLASS: Chondrichthyes.

THRIPS, minute, slender bodied, elongated insects of the order Thysanoptera, the name of the order being derived from the Greek for 'fringed wing', from the fringe of hairs on each side of the four narrow, membranous wings, although some species are wingless. All have short six- to ten-segmented antennae and piercing and sucking asymmetrical mouthparts. Most species are plant feeders, some often being abundant inside flowers, but some are predaceous on other small arthropods.

There are about 4,000 known species,

A typical thrips (order Thysanoptera).

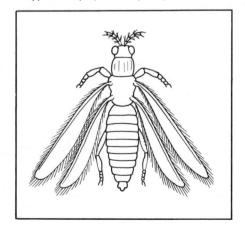

The Thresher shark *Alopias vulpinus* uses the enormous upper lobe of the tail fin to thresh the water and concentrate shoals of fishes before it charges into the middle and seizes its prey.

mostly in the tropics and subtropics. Some are notorious pests, including the Onion thrips *Thrips tabaci,* a pest of onions and many other plants, and the Grain thrips *Limothrips cerealium,* a pest of cereals and grasses.

The order Thysanoptera is divided into two suborders, the Terebrantia and Tubulifera. The female adults of the Terebrantia have a saw-like egg laying organ, the ovipositor. The female cuts slits with the ovipositor and lays her eggs in the tissues of the host plant. The ovipositor is absent in the Tubulifera, and the females of this suborder lay their eggs on the surfaces of leaves or stems.

The nymphs resemble the adults in general character and feeding habits, but are devoid of wings. There are two active nymphal stages or instars, followed by a sedentary non-feeding prepupal and pupal stage in the Terebrantia; in the Tubulifera there are two pupal stages. The pupa moults to give the adult, the time for development from egg to adult usually taking about 25–40 days.

Thrips, especially the Onion thrips, are the vectors of Tomato spotted wilt virus, which infects many plant species in different parts of the world. ORDER: Thysanoptera, CLASS: Insecta, PHYLUM: Arthropoda.   A.J.C.

THRUSHES, slender-billed songbirds of small to medium size. The plumage is most often grey or brown but is sometimes chestnut, blue, green black or pale buff. Some thrushes have long pointed wings, some short rounded wings, with many intermediates. The tail is usually rounded or square, occasionally rather strongly graduated, and it is held erect in some species.

The thrush subfamily, the Turdinae, is distributed throughout the world, with the greatest number and variety in Africa, Asia and Europe. There have been several invasions of thrush-like birds into Australia and New Guinea and into the New World. Thrushes have become isolated on islands for example on Tristan da Cunha and Hawaii, where they have developed into distinctive forms. There are about 300 species, combined into two groups, the 'true thrushes'

centred on the genera *Turdus* and *Zoothera,* and the large varied group of chats.

The genus *Turdus* includes about 63 species. European species include the black-bird *T. merula,* the Song thrush *T. philomelos,* the Mistle thrush *T. viscivorus* and the Ring ouzel *T. torquatus.* It also includes the American robin *T. migratorius* a common garden bird in the United States. Thrushes of the genus *Zoothera* are closely related to those in the genus *Turdus* but they have more rounded wings and white bases to the wing feathers. Most are found only in tropical Asia, but White's thrush *Z. dauma* reaches Europe and several species are found only in the New World, including the Varied thrush *Z. naevia* of the western United States and the Aztec thrush *Z. pinicola* of South America. The Forest thrushes of the Caribbean islands *Cichlherminia* and the Tristan da Cunha thrush *Nesocichla eremita* are offshoots of this group, as are the American genera *Catharus* and *Hylocichla.* These last are two genera of small, slender thrushes found in woodland, scrub and gardens. The Hermit thrush *C. guttata,* the veery *C. fuscescens* and the Wood thrush *H. mustelina* are familiar birds in North America. Old World members of this group include the Blue whistling thrush *Myiophoneus caeruleus* a medium-sized dark blue thrush of southeastern Asia, and the Rock thrushes of the genus *Monticola.* The Rock thrush *M. saxatilis* is a rather small, stocky thrush with rufous and blue plumage and the Blue rock thrush *M. solitarius* is bright, dark blue all over. Both are found in southern Europe and the Near East.

The chats are confined to the Old World. In general they have weaker, less melodious songs, and more slender legs than the true thrushes, and many of them are smaller. European chats include the robin *Erithacus rubecula,* the redstart *Phoenicurus phoenicurus,* Black redstart *P. ochrurus,* wheatear *Oenanthe oenanthe,* stonechat *Saxicola torquata,* the whinchat *S. rubetra* and the nightingale *Luscinia megarhynchos* which is exceptional for this group in having a loud, clear song. The chat group is found in Europe, Asia and Africa. As with the true thrushes, many chats migrate long distances between their breeding and wintering grounds, although some are sedentary throughout the year. Wheatears from Iceland and Greenland migrate over the open Atlantic Ocean to wintering grounds in Africa, and redstarts from northern Europe leave the woodlands where they breed to spend the winter in Central Africa.

The brightly coloured bluebirds of North America are chats, with bright blue plumage. They are found mainly in open country. Other distinctive groups are the shortwings *Brachypteryx* and the genus *Zeledonia*. The former are sedentary, round-winged birds found in the dense jungles of southern Asia. The latter has only one species found in western Panama and Costa Rica in Central America. It is peculiar in possessing only ten instead of 12 tail feathers.

Many distinctive groups of chats are found both in Africa and Asia. In Africa the robin-chats or Forest robins *Alethe* and *Cossypha* are brightly coloured forest birds, and in southern Asia the members of the genus *Copsychus* are familiar songbirds with blue or black plumage.

Most thrushes and chats defend territories in the breeding season. True thrushes sing from perches and chats sing from perches and during display flights. Some species defend territories through the winter, as well as in the breeding season, although winter and summer territories may be different. The territorial instincts of some chats are so strong that they defend territories for even a few days while they are resting on migration. Migrant wheatears are sometimes grounded in large numbers by adverse weather and they can be seen in rows on the tops of stone walls, each bird singing only a few yards away from its neighbour.

Nearly all the 'true thrushes' nest in bushes or trees, building rounded cup-nests of grass, leaves and other materials. The chats have more varied nesting arrangements: some nest in tree or rock holes, some in partially enclosed hollows and some in the open but surrounded by thick vegetation. The colour of the eggs varies in relation to the kind of nest site that is used. The hole nesting species such as the redstart and wheatear lay pale blue or white eggs without markings, those nesting in partially enclosed sites lay pale-coloured eggs with spots and blotches and those nesting in the open lay darker eggs that are more heavily marked. The eggs of the nightingale are so heavily blotched that they appear a uniform dull green, matching the dark background where they are laid.

In those species that have been studied, the female undertakes all the incubation and she is given food at the nest by the male in a few species such as the European robin. Incubation periods vary from 13–15 days and the young of most species hatch with a covering of down, which is dark-coloured in the species nesting in the open. The young are fed by both parents and leave the nest after a period of 12–16 days. After they fledge the young are often fed by their parents for several weeks.

Most of the chats eat mainly insects but also take spiders, tiny reptiles, worms, snails and other animals. Some of the true thrushes subsist mainly on worms and snails but many of them take fruit and berries in the autumn and winter, sometimes to the exclusion of other foods. FAMILY: Muscicapidae, ORDER: Passeriformes, CLASS: Aves.   D.H.

Blue Whistling thrush *Myiophoneus caeruleus*, of southeastern Asia, also known as the Whistling Schoolboy.

Opposite: the fieldfare *Turdus pilaris*, a large member of the thrush family, breeds in northern Europe and moves southwards in autumn.

THRUSH STORM-COCK. The Mistle thrush *Turdus viscivorus*, sometimes spelt missel thrush, is a large songbird of the thrush subfamily, found in Europe and parts of western Asia. Greyish-brown above, spotted beneath, this bird derives its name from its habit of feeding on mistletoe berries. It is also called 'storm-cock' because, unlike most birds, it frequently sings in rough weather. It has been seen singing in a blizzard or in a half-gale of wind perched at the top of a sapling and in full song while the sapling was whipped back and forth by the wind.

THUNDERWORM *Mermis,* one of the *roundworms. It lives, when young, parasitically in grasshoppers, ants and other insects feeding on their internal organs. In summer, when adult, threadlike and up to 20 in (50 cm) long, *Mermis* may be found coiled like a tangle of cotton in the topsoil or climbing fully extended over plants, especially rose bushes, after heavy rain or a thunderstorm. ORDER: Mermithoidea, CLASS: Nematoda, PHYLUM: Aschelminthes.

THYLACINE *Thylacinus cynocephalus,* the alternative name for the Tasmanian or *Marsupial wolf.

TIBETAN ANTELOPE *Pantholops hodgsoni,* or *chiru, the goat-antelope of the Tibetan plateau.

TICKS, annoying parasites of man and domestic animals the importance of which in disease transmission did not become apparent until just prior to the opening of the present century. Studies then which implicated ticks as vectors of a protozoan disease of cattle, Texas cattle fever, focused world attention on the potential danger of this group of arthropods.

The subclass Acari, which contains both mites and ticks, differs from most arthropods since the body is not divided. A true head is lacking and the thorax and abdomen are fused producing a sac-like appearance. Ticks should not be confused with the wingless insects such as the Sheep ked, often referred to as the 'Sheep tick'. The suborder Ixodides, which comprises the ticks, differs from the suborders of mites by their larger size, the presence of a pair of breathing pores, or spiracles, behind the third or fourth pair of legs, and by having a unique type of sensory organ (Hallar's organ) situated on the distal segment of each of the first pair of legs.

In place of a true head, ticks have a gnathosoma bearing the mouthparts. It consists of a basal portion, a pair of four-segmented palps and a rigid holdfast organ, usually toothed, called the hypostome which serves to anchor the parasite to its host. In addition, a pair of cutting organs or chelicerae permit the tick to cut the skin for the penetration of the hypostome.

The 700 species of ticks are all blood-sucking, external parasites of vertebrates including amphibians, reptiles, birds and mammals. Because of this specialized way of life they have several special adaptations, one of which is a powerful sucking pharynx. After the chelicerae have broken the skin of the host the hypostome is inserted into the wound and the tick commences feeding. The salivary glands of some ticks produce secretions that prevent blood from coagulating and the blood is pumped in by the pharynx and forced back into the oesophagus, stomach and diverticula of the stomach. The body of ticks is covered with a leathery cuticle capable of great distension as the blood is being forced into the diverticula of the stomach. Unengorged ticks of different species vary tremendously in size (1–30 mm). Some species are capable of ingesting hundreds of times their weight in blood and after engorgement they may attain a size many times greater than when unengorged.

Ticks have four stages in their life-cycle: the egg, a 6-legged larva and an 8-legged nymph and adult.

There are three families of ticks, the Argasidae, Ixodidae and Nuttalliellidae. The last contains only one species, *Nuttalliella namaqua,* collected in Little Namaqualand, Republic of South Africa. This tick is extremely rare and is of no medical or economic importance. However, members of both the family Argasidae and the family Ixodidae are numerous and of great medical and economic importance. In fact, ticks transmit more diseases to man and domestic animals than any other group of arthropods except mosquitoes.

The Argasidae, with 95 species, commonly known as soft ticks or argasids, differ greatly from the Ixodidae. The sexes are similar, they lack a sclerotized dorsal plate (scutum), and the gnathosoma is located ventrally in the nymph and adult. The integument of all stages except the larva is leathery, wrinkled, granulated, mammillated, or with tubercules. The integument of the larvae is much thinner and except for setae lacks noticeable wrinkles and protuberances.

Argasid ticks frequent nests, dens and resting places of their hosts. Some feed on humans whereas others attack birds, bats and other small mammals. They can go for extended periods, even years, without feeding. There are records of adult ticks being kept alive for 40 years while being fed only at 5-year intervals.

Adults of soft ticks are typically intermittent feeders, and eggs are laid a few at a time in areas where the females seek shelter. The larval feeding period varies from a few minutes to several days. Larvae detach after feeding and moult into the nymphal stage. There are often several successive nymphal feedings and subsequent moultings into a more advanced nymphal stage before transformation to the adult stage occurs.

Several species of argasid ticks are of medical or veterinary importance. The Fowl tick *Argas persicus* is a serious pest of poultry in a number of regions around the world. In many places it is a vector of fowl spirochaetosis, a disease with a high mortality rate. This tick will parasitize man and often attacks poultry workers.

The Spinose ear tick *Otobius megnini* feeds deep in the ears of domestic and wild animals in semi-arid regions throughout the world. The nymph is covered with spines and heavy infestations of this tick in the ears of animals can produce an intense irritation, unthriftiness or even death.

A number of species of the genus *Ornithodoros* transmit relapsing fever to man on every continent, with the possible exception of Australia and Antarctica. All of these species are commonly referred to as Relapsing fever ticks. In Africa *O. moubata* transmits this disease, whereas the important vectors in the Western Hemisphere are *O. turicata, O. hermsi, O. talaje* and *O. rudis*. In Asia an important vector of this relapsing fever is *O. tholozani*.

The bites of many of the species of soft ticks may produce local and systemic reactions in humans. For example, the bites of *O. coriaceus* of California and Mexico are extremely venomous.

In the Ixodidae or hard ticks, with 550 species, the sexes are markedly dissimilar. This is partly due to the presence of a tough dorsal covering (dorsal plate or scutum) on at least a portion of the body of all Ixodidae. The scutum covers the entire dorsal surface of the males, while it is present only on the front part of the female, nymph and larval stage. It may be brightly coloured or dull brown or black. Further, the gnathosoma extends forward in hard ticks, and large spiracles are located behind the hindlegs in adults and nymphal hard ticks.

Although some species of hard ticks frequent nests and animal resting places, many more tend to be randomly distributed throughout the hosts' environment. Larvae, nymphs and adults feed only once, and several days are usually required for them to complete feeding. After the female has fed, mated and dropped to the ground she lays a mass containing up to 10,000 or more eggs. These hatch and the larvae then seek to attach to a suitable host. If the larva is successful in finding a host it feeds and usually drops to the ground and moults into a nymph. The nymph must then find another animal and if successful will feed, drop to the ground and moult into an adult. Then the adult must attach to a host and feed and mate to begin the life-cycle again.

This typical three-host life-cycle is not common to all species of hard ticks. For

example, all species of the genus *Boophilus* attach to a host as larvae and all subsequent feedings and moultings take place on this same host animal. Fully engorged females drop off the host and lay their eggs on the ground. Species with this sort of life-cycle are referred to as one-host ticks. Still another variation is found in other ixodid species, typified by the Red-legged tick *Rhipicephalus evertsi*. In this instance the larval feeding, larval moult and nymphal feeding occur on the same host and then engorged nymphs drop to the ground and transform into adults. Ticks that utilize two animals for the completion of their life-cycle are called two-host ticks.

Many species of hard ticks are also of great medical and veterinary importance, by transmitting a variety of disease agents to man and animals and causing considerable economic loss by the effects of their bite on livestock. It has been estimated that as much as 200 pounds of blood may be withdrawn from a large, heavily infested host-animal during a single season. In addition, the bites also cause other disorders such as dermatosis and systemic disturbances due to the inoculation of toxic substances. Certain species cause a form of paralysis which, though infrequent, is often fatal and affects humans and a variety of domestic animals and pets.

The kinds of disease agents transferred by ixodid ticks include viruses, rickettsia, bacteria, and Protozoa. Transmission occurs when the tick bites the host or, in certain instances, when crushed tick tissues or excrement contacts skin or skin lesions. Viruses transmitted by ixodid ticks include Colorado tick fever, a disease of man in the western United States transmitted primarily by the Rocky Mountain *wood tick *Dermacentor andersoni,* louping ill, a disease of sheep in the British Isles vectored by the European Castor bean tick *Ixodes ricinus,* Russian spring-summer encephalitis and related diseases in Europe and Asia primarily transmitted by the European Castor bean tick and the Taiga tick *Ixodes persulcatus,* and Kyasanur Forest disease carried by *Haemaphysalis spinigera.* Some important rickettsial diseases of man are Rocky Mountain spotted fever, widely distributed in the Western Hemisphere and, in North America, chiefly vectored by the American dog tick *Dermacentor variabilis* and the Rocky Mountain wood tick, boutonneuse fever and some related diseases of the Mediterranean region and Africa, which are transmitted by the Brown dog tick *Rhipicephalus sanguineus.* A bacterial disease, tularaemia (rabbit fever), is transmitted by several species of hard ticks in the Northern Hemisphere.

The numerous tick-borne diseases of dom-

A female tick, fully fed and bloated with eggs.

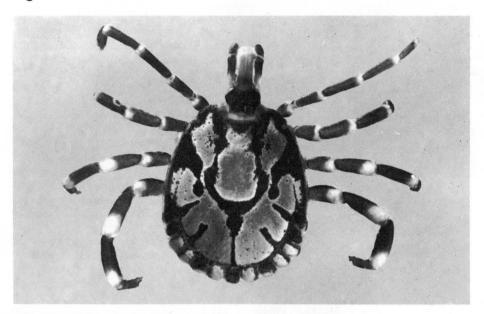

An ixodid or Hard tick, the male of the **Bont tick** *Amblyomma hebraeum.*

estic animals cause vast economic losses in tropical and subtropical areas. Some examples are: babesiosis, caused by species of the protozoan *Babesia* and transmitted principally by Cattle ticks of the genus *Boophilus,* and East Coast fever, also a protozoan disease in Africa, caused by *Theileria parva,* which is vectored by several species of the genus *Rhipicephalus.*

The list of diseases given above is by no means complete. Only a few of the more important diseases transmitted by soft and hard ticks have been discussed.

To achieve effective control of a parasite sufficient knowledge of the morphology of the species on a given area must be available to allow their identification so control efforts will not be wasted on wrong or unimportant species. Further, a body of information on the habits of important species must be collected so that the control measures can be applied to the most vulnerable stage in the life-cycle.

Control of ticks on livestock is usually undertaken by applying one or more of a variety of insecticides, administered as dusts, dips, sprays or more recently by incorporating the insecticide in the feed given to animals. These should not be used without first getting the advice of a veterinarian or competent health official.

In certain areas such as recreational sites, control of ticks on the ground or foliage is desirable and may be accomplished by insecticide treatment. However, such treatment should be preceded by an intensive survey of an area to determine the abundance, seasonal occurrence and distribution of the species, since without this knowledge the control measures will most likely be ineffective and expensive. Area control is more posssible with species that inhabit restricted areas such as roadsides, caves or buildings. In area control it may be helpful to reduce the animal populations that feed the various stages of the tick by means of poisoned bait. This technique should be undertaken with caution since if certain ticks are deprived of their usual hosts they may turn on humans for their blood supply.

In regions where ticks are known to transmit diseases to humans it is best to avoid these areas during the season when ticks are active and abundant. If this is not practical some measure of protection can be afforded by wearing suitable clothing such as high boots or by tucking trouser legs into the tops of socks. Before retiring at night, or after leaving an infested area a careful search of the body should be made for the presence of ticks. It is important to remove the ticks as soon as possible since ticks cannot transmit some diseases without a certain period of attachment. Further, certain chemicals such as diethyltoluomide, dimethylphthalate and ethylhexanediol applied to clothing have been effective in repelling ticks.

Once a tick is attached there have been a number of methods proposed for their removal such as burning them with the lighted end of a cigarette, and applying nail polish or a variety of other chemicals. However, in most instances they may easily be removed by gently pulling the tick off with the fingers. Unfortunately this method of removing ticks may break off the mouthparts of some species with longer hypostomes. When sterile instruments are available they can be removed by pulling on the tick to elevate the skin surrounding the site of attachment and then slipping the point of a needle or scalpel under the mouthparts. With gentle pressure the mouthparts can be removed with a minimum of tissue damage. Once the tick is removed an antiseptic should be applied. ORDER: Metastigmata, SUBCLASS: Acari, CLASS: Arachnida, PHYLUM: Arthropoda.   C.M.C.

TIGER *Panthera tigris,* the major feline of the Asian continent. A number of attempts to separate the races of tiger into different species have been abortive and it is now accepted that all tigers belong to one species. There is a close link with lions, and the two will interbreed in captivity to give fertile young. The cubs being known as 'tiglons' or 'ligers', the first syllable of the name coming from the male parent. The cubs take on some characteristics of each parent.

Tigers are the largest of the cats, but they are slimmer and narrower in the body than lions, and only an expert can distinguish between the skeletons of the two species. That of the tiger provides support for the powerful muscles of the hindquarters for the spring, and strength to the forelimbs for gripping and dragging down prey. The coat provides a natural camouflage against the patterns of light and shade in the natural surroundings, and it is said that a running tiger in the jungle looks grey against the background. Regardless of race, the coat usually has the same basic colouring, the ground colour being a shade of reddish fawn, broken at intervals by dark vertical stripes. The belly is white and there are patches of white on the face. The claws are hooked and retractile and the teeth are used for the holding, tearing and cutting of flesh, the staple diet. In terms of both armament and camouflage, the tiger is one of the best equipped of all the carnivores.

The various races of tiger vary enormously in colour, size and weight, but they all follow the same basic patterns of build and the colour combinations are easy to recognize. The only real exception is the White tiger of Rewa. In this form, the ground colour of the coat is a shade of cream, marked with light charcoal or milk-chocolate stripes. The eyes are blue and the pads and nose are pink. These animals are an 'extreme dilute', rather than an albino form. They are born in the same litter as normal cubs, but they appear to be rather more robust. There are only two cases of true albino tigers on record. There are, however, many pictures of black tigers, but the generally accepted explanation is that a tiger, when it is feeding on a large carcass, such as a buffalo, may become covered in blood, giving a very black appearance when it dries.

Fossils show that the tiger originated in Siberia and the New Siberian Islands and then spread south to occupy most of Asia and parts of the Malaysian Archipelago. The northern-most race still lives in Siberia, Manchuria and North Korea. Tigers shed their coats seasonally and are intolerant of great heat, indicating that they originated in a colder climate.

Opposite: *tigress carrying young in mouth.*

Tigers mating. A characteristic of the mating behaviour of felines is that the male seizes the female's neck with his teeth.

They become mature at three years of age, and for about the next eleven years, a tigress will mate approximately every two to two and a half years. The interval is devoted to the rearing and training of the previous litter. In captivity, tigers will breed more frequently, as there is no need to train the cubs. The gestation period is 105–115 days, and a litter consists of two to six young, but only one, or perhaps two of the cubs will ever reach maturity. The tigress herself controls the size of the litter to some extent by 'weeding out' the sickly and injured young. The cubs are blind at birth, but have a fully marked coat and weigh from 2–3 lb (1–1·5 kg). By the time they are six weeks old, the cubs will have been weaned, and at the age of seven months, they will have

started to kill for themselves. In spite of the fact that the mortality rate in an individual litter is so high, a tigress may still leave up to 20 descendants. The males are polygamous, and play little or no part in the rearing of the young, although they may hunt with the mother, thus indirectly contributing to the supply of food.

For the most part, tigers are solitary, although they may occasionally hunt as a pair, one animal driving the prey down to the ambush formed by the hunting partner. Although tigers belong to the so called 'roaring cats', they do not roar as much as lions, doing so only briefly when charging or threatening. A surprised tiger will give a 'whoof' of alarm before making off. Another sound has been described as 'belling' be-

cause of the similarity to the noise made by the Sambar stag. This sound indicates alarm or uneasiness. Finally, there is a moaning or mewing sound made when the tiger is moving through cover. This appears to be the same as the purr of the domestic cat and may indicate contentment and satisfaction.

Tigers have been classed as mainly nocturnal cats, but this is not necessarily so. They avoid the heat of the day, and will often lie in water to keep cool. They are excellent swimmers. Preferring to hunt in the cool of the day, they will take a variety of prey from wild pig to buffalo. In times of food shortage, they have been known to eat lizards, frogs and even crocodiles. The tigers of India also appear to have a fondness for the Durian fruit. All tigers will eat carrion

Tiger lying at ease in the shade.

and will return to a kill a number of times. A full grown tiger will eat 40–60 lb (18–27 kg) of meat at one feed in the wild. A probable average intake would be about 20 lb (9 kg) per day, involving the killing of 45–50 deer a year.

Smaller prey, such as the Wild pig, is attacked from the front with a leap, the forelimbs seizing the neck of the prey and pulling it to the ground. Larger animals, like buffalo, may be hamstrung from behind before the tiger leaps onto the animal's back, and, gripping its neck with the front legs and claws, throws it, often breaking its neck in the process. Tigers do not undertake long chases after food, but prefer to stalk and spring. In this, the natural camouflage is particularly effective and even a large tiger

can move through very low cover unobserved. When the kill has been made, the tiger may drag the prey to a place of safety which is usually heavily screened, before starting to feed. It follows a definite routine in feeding, starting at the hindquarters and working its way forward to the head during successive feeds. Tigers show remarkable strength in pulling a carcass, and a well-grown male has been observed pulling a pig weighing 200 lb (90 kg) more than half a mile.

The Siberian tiger *Panthera tigris altaica* is not only the largest of the tigers, but it is also the largest of the cats. A full grown male may weigh as much as 640 lb (290 kg) and may be as long as 13 ft (4 m) overall. It is probable that this race is the closest to the

original stock, for they were once widely distributed throughout Siberia, Manchuria and North and South Korea, but now they are found only in the Russian reserves of Sudzuhke and Sikhote Alin, the Mount Baekdu Highlands and the Machonryung and Rangrim ranges of North Korea and the Changpai and Lesser Hsingan mountains of Manchuria. There are about 200 in the wild. In overall colouring they are lighter than the Bengal tiger, which is the typical race and they have fewer and less noticeable stripes. The belly and face also have considerable areas of white. The winter coat is long and shaggy, to withstand temperatures of −40°F (−40°C), while the summer coat is shorter and darker, although it still tends to be heavier than in tigers elsewhere.

The Chinese tiger *P. tigris amoyensis* is now very rare, but was once widespread throughout South China and overlapped in some areas with the Bengal race.

It is from the Bengal tiger *P. tigris tigris* that the species receives its name. Found in India from the Himalayas to the South, it has shorter hair and is more brightly coloured. A male can weigh 420 lb (190 kg) and measure 9·5 ft (2·8 m). The females, as is the case with all tigers, weigh about 100–150 lb (45–68 kg) less.

The Caspian tiger *P. tigris virgata*, well represented until recent times, is now found in only a few localities along the Caspian, in the Caucasus, the Karakals and in northern Afghanistan. It is slightly smaller than the Bengal race and has a thicker coat and paler stripes. It is now extensively hunted for its skin, which fetches a high price. It is remarkable for its extreme wandering habit.

The beautifully coloured Sumatran tiger *P. tigris sumatrae* is the smallest of the races, measuring only 29 in (75 cm) at the shoulder. It is darker than the others and is more heavily striped. The ground colour is a rich orange with broader and darker stripes. The white areas of the other races have become buff on the face and belly. It is now to be found only in two regions of Sumatra; the mountainous area of the southwest, and in parts of the northern part of the island. It was well represented until the Second World War, but since then hunting and trapping have made heavy inroads into the population. It is regularly hunted by hunters from Java.

Native only to Java, the Java tiger *P. tigris sondaica* is now found only in the reserves of Udjong Kulon and Betiri. It is thought that this animal may have reached Java by swimming and indeed it has been observed swimming channels 3 miles (5 km) wide without apparent difficulty. Slightly larger than the Sumatran race, it has a similar bright colouration. It has been brought to the verge of extinction by uncontrolled hunting and trapping but has been bred successfully in zoos.

It is possible that the Bali tiger *P. tigris balica* was introduced to Bali from Java by man. It has, nonetheless, certain racial characteristics that set it apart from the others. It is extremely rare and there are probably not more than about ten living at the moment. It will probably soon become extinct. FAMILY: Felidae, ORDER: Carnivora, CLASS: Mammalia.   N.J.C.

TIGER BEETLES, popular name for a group of beetles, which is well deserved since they are formidable predators with large sharply toothed jaws, probably the most voracious

A Tiger beetle *Megacephala denticollis* of Nigeria dismembering a grasshopper.

Two tigerfish leaping from the waters of the Niger River, above the Kainji Dam, Nigeria.

and ferocious of insects, especially as larvae. Their eyes are large, their legs are long, and they run and fly quickly. Their habit is to run speedily when disturbed, then take to the wing and fly for about 50 ft (15 m) before again alighting on the ground. There are about 2,000 species, typically 1 in (2·5 cm) long, mostly in the warmer parts of the world. They are often common in sandy areas near the sea, or on lake shores. Some species are found on riverbanks and others live on dry heathland. Many of the species are most active in the middle of the day in the hot sun, but there are also a few nocturnal species. Their colours are often bright particularly the upper surface of the abdomen, which is exposed in flight.

The larva has a large flattened head, and lives in a vertical shaft in the ground where it waits for passing prey which it seizes with its large jaws. FAMILY: Cicindelidae, ORDER: Coleoptera, CLASS: Insecta, PHYLUM: Arthropoda.

TIGERFISHES, African freshwater fishes of the genus *Hydrocynus,* deriving their common name from their striped colouring and voracious appetite. The body is elongated and powerful and the mouth is armed with curved, dagger-like teeth. These fishes prey chiefly on other fishes and the largest species, *H. goliath,* which reaches 125 lb (56 kg) in weight, has been suspected of attacking cattle and even human beings. Fish eaten by the tigerfishes are either swallowed whole or have the soft parts cleanly bitten off.

Young tigerfishes shoal in shallow waters but larger fishes are mostly solitary, living in deeper water. Because of the importance of freshwater fishes as a source of protein in Africa, the tigerfishes have been the subject of various investigations, both as a source of food and because of their effect as predators on other useful species. It has been found that *H. vittatus* reaches its peak of efficiency as a predator on other fishes when it is 12–18 in (30–45 cm) long. Fishes smaller than this catch less relative to their body weight, while larger fishes also catch less because their bodies are fatter and their fins relatively smaller and they are thus less efficient swimmers. It is factors such as this that may set the limit on the maximum size to which such fishes can grow.

The tigerfishes are found in the Nile and in those rivers and lakes which once had a connection with the Nile. They are absent from Lake Victoria and the eastward-flowing rivers of East Africa, presumably because these were never in contact with the Nile system (the Murchison Falls presenting an absolute barrier to the passage of Nile fishes into Lake Victoria). FAMILY: Characidae, ORDER: Cypriniformes, CLASS: Pisces.

TIGER SNAKES, a group of closely related Australian *elapid snakes of the genus *Notechis.* All are restricted to the coast, ranges and wetter parts of the interior of southern Australia, including Tasmania.

They are relatively heavy, thick bodied snakes with broad, rather massive heads. The Common tiger snake of southeastern Australia, *N. scutatus,* averages only a little over 4 ft (1·2 m) and varies considerably in colour and pattern. It ranges through various shades of grey, brown, reddish or olive to almost black. Typically it has numerous light yellowish cross-bands along its length, but these are often indistinct or absent.

A number of isolated populations of Tiger snakes are variously regarded either as distinct species or as geographic variations of a single species. The most distinctive of these populations occur on various small islands in Bass Strait and off the coast of South Australia. These insular Tiger snakes are generally characterized by melanism, an excessive development of black pigment resulting in snakes which are uniform dark brown or black above and cream to dark grey below, although in many specimens a faint banded pattern persists. The black Tiger snakes of the islands of eastern Bass Strait differ from all others by their larger size, for they average nearly 6 ft (1·8 m) in length and may reach a length of 8 ft (2·4 m).

In southwestern Australia is another isolated Tiger snake population. This Western tiger snake *N. scutatus occidentalis* grows to 7 ft (2·2 m) in length, although it averages only about 4½ ft (1·3 m). It is very dark grey to black above, with or without numerous narrow yellowish cross-bands, while the belly is yellowish to grey.

Tiger snakes are normally shy and inoffensive, but react savagely when provoked. The neck is then flattened like that of a cobra while the first quarter or so of the flattened body is held off the ground in a long, low arc. All are highly venomous, their venoms being among the most potent known. Although they have

A Tiger snake trying to eat a frog the wrong way round. The snake's eye is green as it is sloughing its skin.

relatively short, immovable fangs they cause a high proportion of the average of only four deaths which result from snake-bite in Australia each year. Before the development of an antivenine in 1929, the first to be developed for any Australian snake, about 45% of Tiger snake victims died. Like that of other dangerous Australian elapids, the venom of Tiger snakes acts largely on the central nervous system, causing death by respiratory paralysis. The potency of Tiger snake venom varies considerably in different populations, the most potent yet recorded being that from the Black tiger snake *N. ater,* from Reevesby Island in Spencer Gulf, South Australia. It was found to have venom more than twice as deadly as that of Tiger snakes from the mainland of southeastern Australia.

Tiger snakes are found in a wide variety of habitats. In southern Queensland they chiefly inhabit rain-forests, whereas in the southern part of their range they are generally found in wet coastal scrubs and sclerophyl forests. West of the Great Dividing Range they often occur in dense colonies along river banks and flood plains, or around large swamps and lakes. Although frogs constitute the principal source of food, small mammals, birds, lizards and, on occasion, fish are also eaten. For Tiger snakes from the Bass Strait islands, the chicks of the muttonbird or Sooty shearwater

Puffinus tenuirostris are eaten, while their nesting burrows are utilized for shelter. The Western tiger snake is said to inhabit most damp environments within its range.

Tiger snakes produce living young, an average litter numbering about 50. The young measure about 8 in (20 cm) at birth, and are usually much more strongly banded than the adults. FAMILY: Elapidae, ORDER: Squamata, CLASS: Reptilia.   H.G.C.

TILAPIA, perch-like fishes of the genus *Tilapia,* found principally in Africa but occurring also in Lake Tiberias and other water masses connected with the northern extension of the African Rift Valley. Species of *Tilapia* are found in lakes, streams and rivers, but some will penetrate into brackish waters. Typically, the body is fairly deep and compressed, with a long dorsal fin (the anterior rays being spiny) and a moderate anal fin. In some species a black spot occurs on the hind part of the dorsal fin, occasionally edged in yellow. This 'Tilapia mark' is not always retained in the adults. Teeth are present in the jaws and also in the throat, the pharyngeal tooth pads associated with the bones of the fifth gill arch. Although the form of the pharyngeal teeth may sometimes vary with the type of food available to individual populations of the same species, the teeth are

usually diagnostic of the species or species group and are of great use in identifications. Members of this genus have successfully invaded a wide range of habitats but are principally found in lakes where they form the basis for large local fisheries. Certain dwarfed species, such as *T. grahami* of Lake Magadi, Kenya, have become adapted to highly alkaline hot springs, while others, for example *T. spilurus,* are typically found in rivers. In good growing conditions, many species will reach at least 12 in (30 cm) and in Lake Rudolf, Kenya, specimens of *T. nilotica* weighing 14 lb (6·3 kg) have been recorded. Many species of *Tilapia* have been described but their identification is often extremely difficult, depending to some extent on male breeding colouration which has usually faded by the time that the specimens can be examined in a laboratory or museum.

Many species of *Tilapia* are *mouth-brooders. At the onset of the breeding season the male becomes more highly coloured and establishes a territory, usually in shallow water over sand or mud. The male then excavates a nest, a shallow circular depression 12 in (30 cm) or more in diameter, taking material in the mouth from the centre and spitting it out beyond the rim of the nest. When the nest is complete, the male guards it from intruding males or members of other species by a series of postures and swimming antics, but will go through a special ritual if a female of its own species approaches the nest. When the female has laid the eggs at the bottom of the nest, the male discharges sperm over them and the eggs and sperm are taken into the mouth of the female. In some species it is the male that takes up the eggs. The female mouth-brooder then leaves the nest, or is chased away, and thereafter broods the eggs until they hatch, which happens after about 5 days. Even then the fry are retained in the mouth of the parent for some days and even when they venture forth in a little cloud they will swim back into the safety of the mouth if alarmed. In some species it has been noticed that the fry will 'freeze' at the sudden appearance of a predator while the parent deals with the danger. While brooding the young, the parent is unable to feed.

In a few species of *Tilapia* the eggs are left within the nest to incubate. In *T. zillii,* for example, the eggs are laid in the nest and fertilized and thereafter are fanned by the pectoral fins of both parents. The parents take eggs which have failed to hatch into their mouths and deposit them outside the nest. They also do the same with the hatched larvae. The larvae are equipped with a gland in the head from which a sticky thread is secreted. The thread adheres to the bottom and prevents the larva from drifting away.

Because of their hardiness and palatability, species of *Tilapia* have been widely used in fish culture in ponds. They breed freely under such conditions but this has proved to be a drawback since the resultant over-population produces stunting. Experiments using *T. spilurus* in Kenya have shown that a breeding population in a ¼ acre (0·1 ha) pond will produce fishes of 6 in (15 cm) while a controlled population of 200 fishes will grow to 12 in (30 cm). The control of pond populations by stocking males only was pioneered by Dr V. D. van Someren, who showed that in certain species the male grows faster than the female.

One of the most popular species grown in ponds is *T. mossambica,* a species found in parts of eastern Africa but now widely distributed throughout the tropical regions of the world. In 1939 a few specimens were found by Pak Mudjair in eastern Java and were dubbed Ikan mudjair or Mudjair's fish. No one has yet discovered how they got there. By 1943 they had been introduced into many parts of Indonesia and also into Malaya. In 1949 Malayan specimens were taken to St Lucia in the West Indies, arriving appropriately enough on St Peter's day. In 1951 other Malayan fishes were taken to Ceylon and from there were introduced into India and Pakistan. By 1955 they had been introduced into Egypt, not from Africa but from Thailand, which they had reached in 1944. By 1954 they were in Japan and they are now found in Florida and Texas. Dr James Atz finally documented the story of the peregrinating *Tilapia,* but many fisheries' biologists have been worried by the possible effects of *Tilapia* on natural stocks in rivers and lakes.

The two species most often imported for aquarists are *T. zillii* and *T. tholloni.* Both are plant-eaters and should not be put into tanks containing expensive water plants. FAMILY: Cichlidae, ORDER: Perciformes, CLASS: Pisces.

Tilapia tholloni male in breeding dress – the red on throat and belly – in the act of digging a pit in the sand.

TILAPIA DRAUGHTS. Some of the miracles described in the Bible have been explained as being no more than embroidered accounts of natural phenomena. It has, for instance, been suggested that the story of the miraculous draught of fishes is a not unusual occurrence in the Sea of Galilee. There are several species of *Tilapia* living in this inland sea and *T. galilaea* is found in shoals each covering an acre. It is the custom of the fishermen to station a man on a high point of the shore who can detect shoals swimming just beneath the surface and guide the fishermen in their boats to the shoals. These are so tightly packed that it is possible to find no fish on one side of a boat but to fill a net to breaking point on the other.

TILEFISH *Lopholatilus chamaeleonticeps,* one of the largest members of the family Pseudochromidae, reaching 3 ft (90 cm) in length. It is related to the Sea perches. There is a sharp crest at the back of the head. The body is fairly slender and the anal fin and single dorsal fin are fairly long. The discovery and the subsequent sudden disappearance of the tilefish present a rather curious story. The fish was first discovered in 1879. It was found at the bottom of the Gulf Stream slope of the shores of New England. The water mass in which the tilefishes were found was at that time warm since it was composed of Gulf Stream water that had travelled northwards from the Gulf of Mexico. The fishes were found in large numbers and a fishery subsequently developed. Three years later, after some extremely severe gales, the course of the Gulf Stream altered and the area in which the tilefishes lived was invaded by a much colder body of water from the Labrador Current. For some reason the tilefish is exceedingly sensitive to changes in water temperatures and this sudden cooling was enough to kill off the fishes in millions. In March 1882 an area of some 15,000 sq miles (40,000 sq km) was strewn with dead tilefishes. For the next 20 years no tilefishes were caught and it was presumed that the species was extinct. Then they slowly made a reappearance in the warmer waters of the Gulf Stream and their numbers gradually built up once more. The Pseudochromidae contains species which live in tropical waters and it would seem that the tilefish was able to take advantage of warm bodies of water that had for various reasons become pushed into temperate latitudes. FAMILY: Pseudochromidae, ORDER: Perciformes, CLASS: Pisces.

TIMBER BEETLES, members of one family, the Cerambycidae, one of many families of beetles whose larvae and adults are known to damage timber. Known also as longhorns, *Longhorn beetles or longicorns, because of their long antennae, this family is of the greatest importance. About 20,000 species have already been named and they are to be found throughout the world wherever trees or bushes grow, and wherever timber is transported or used. The number of British indigenous species is between 60 and 70, but a further 46 are to be found from time to time as larvae in imported timber, some of them quite commonly. Well over 1,200 species are known from the Indian region. Although the longhorns are usually rather more than medium size for beetles a number, especially from South America and, to a lesser extent, from Africa, are of gigantic proportions and often they are of remarkable form and they show an infinite variety of colour and pattern.

The great majority of the larvae infest some part of the woody tissue of woody plants. A few species, however, consume the roots, and others the stems, of herbaceous plants. Many species of longhorns attack only one species of plant but some are polyphagous, attacking a large number of plants. One, *Stromatium barbatum,* is known to feed upon 311 different tree species whilst, on the other hand 38 species of Timber beetles are listed as attacking the single tree species *Shorea robusta* (a member of the genus from which the timbers Meranti and Seraya are converted). In Europe and in some other parts of the world, to which it has been transported through commerce, the best-known Timber beetle species and, economically, the most important, is the House longhorn beetle *Hylotrupes bajulus.*

Some species, such as *Macrotoma heros* and *Titanus giganteus,* are amongst the largest known insects, with a body size of about 6 in (15 cm) long. On the other hand, some species are very small and a few are even minute. The most characteristic feature of the longhorns, shared by all but a few species, is the extreme length of the antennae which are usually as long as, or longer than, the body. In *Batocera kiebleri* they reach a length of 9 in (22·5 cm). The eyes are usually large and are frequently bow-shaped. FAMILY: Cerambycidae, ORDER: Coleoptera, CLASS: Insecta, PHYLUM: Arthropoda.   N.E.H.

One of the insect scourges, in Britain at least, is the Death-watch beetle *Xestobium rufovillosum*, which has eaten into the timbers of ancient buildings such as cathedrals, causing extensive damage.

A Timber beetle, or Longhorn beetle, *Acanthophorus maculatus* of Nigeria.

TIME SENSE, shown when animals can learn to perform certain behaviour patterns at particular times of the day. Such a sense was first demonstrated with honeybees when it was realized that they would frequent the place where a tea-table was laid only at the appropriate time of the day. The insects were attracted in the first place to the jam laid on the table. This led to experiments in which food dishes were put out at definite time intervals and the number of visits paid by marked bees to them and to the same place at other times were noted. More visits were paid at the time when food dishes could be expected. This ability does not depend upon the sun for the bees also learned to search for food at certain times when they were confined in a cellar out of sight of the sun. Indeed later experiments showed that bees flown from Europe to New York and

kept in a room identical to that in their European home would still search for food at the correct 'home' time. Thus, whatever was producing the behaviour was unaffected by the change in longitude.

Not only will bees remember the time of feeding but given sugar water at different concentrations at different times of the day they remember the occasions on which they found the greatest concentrations. They can, however, only be trained to come at 24-hour intervals or at multiples of 24 hours. Thus if they are trained to visit at 48 hour intervals, they will also come for food at 24 hours. The time sense, therefore, seems bound up with a 24-hour rhythm. But in ants feeding rhythms with 35-, 21-, 22-, 26- and 27-hour intervals have been set up.

It is plain that this rhythmic behaviour is on a par with the *rhythmic behaviour con-

trolled by an endogenous or internal clock, known in many other animals. In bees, the conclusion was reached that the time sense depended upon the rate of metabolic processes in the body which are unaffected by deep anaesthesia—for this does not alter the bee's ability to return at the correct time—but are influenced by severe cold and carbon-dioxide narcosis both of which cause a bee to arrive late. Metabolism in bees is speeded up by feeding them globulin which brings them to the feeding place before time.

The internal clock of a bee allows it to compensate for the sun's movement and therefore to use the sun as a guide for navigation on the way back to the hive. Indeed a bee has been observed to dance, a method of indicating the direction of the food source to other bees, for a long period after sunset and even in the night it was able

Tinamous are running birds, living mainly in South America, that are believed to be related to ostriches.

to give the bearing of the last food source as if the sun had continued across the sky instead of sinking below the horizon.

The time sense of bees has an important consequence apart from its use in navigation. Nectar flow in many plant species is distinctly rhythmic following a roughly 24-hour cycle. Foraging bees therefore soon learn to visit a patch of flowers only at those times of day when the nectar will be abundant. This is another aspect of the remarkable economy of effort in the foraging bee for wasted visits between times of nectar flow are eliminated.   J.D.C.

TINAMOUS, some 50 species of neotropical birds, pheasant-like in plumage and guinea-fowl-like in form. They fly weakly and with reluctance. This is an indication of their ancestry, for they are almost certainly most closely related to the ratites, the large flightless birds such as the ostrich. They do, however, have flight muscles attached to a keeled sternum. These are of an appreciable size, but the heart and lungs are very small which accounts for the weak flight. Tinamous sometimes fly into obstacles when flushed, occasionally with serious consequences.

Tinamous are efficient running birds and have a well camouflaged plumage of browns and greys, streaked, spotted or barred. They range widely over South America from southern Mexico to Patagonia and from the tropical rain-forests to 14,000 ft (4,200 m) up in the Andes. They vary in length from 8–21 in (20–53 cm). The body is compact, with a very short tail, and the wings are short and rounded. The legs are strong, and the hind toe

is elevated or missing entirely—a tendency followed in many other running birds. The neck is quite long and the head is small but often strikingly marked in black and white, or crested. The bill is rather long and is decurved and pointed for feeding on a variety of plant materials and small animals picked up from the ground. The sexes are rather similar in appearance but the female is usually larger.

Most species are solitary, except during the breeding season when they are polygamous —some polygynous and some polyandrous. The nest is a depression in the ground, poorly lined. The number of eggs in a nest is anything up to 12, the larger clutches probably being laid by more than one female. The colouration of the eggs is remarkable. They are always unmarked with a surface sheen resembling polished metal or porcelain and may be green, blue, yellow, purple, black or chocolate. Incubation is carried out by the male alone and lasts for about 20 days. The young leave the nest with the male in the first day or so after hatching. They run well and, like the adults, crouch when danger threatens and merge with their surroundings. Some species breed throughout the year, while others have a well-defined breeding season.

There are nine genera of tinamous. The Martineta tinamou *Eudromia elegans* is a gregarious species, living in the open tablelands of southern Argentina in coveys of up to a 100 birds. The Ornate tinamou *Nothoprocta ornata,* found from Bolivia to southern Peru in the treeless heights of the Andes, is solitary, being found only singly or in pairs. When breeding, the male performs the display but the female defends the territory. Bona-

parte's tinamou *Nothocercus bonapartei,* found in mountain forests of Colombia and Venezuela, has an intermediate form of social life, each successful male gathering up to three females which all lay in the same nest.

Tinamous are quite palatable and are hunted for their flesh. They breed relatively readily in captivity but have nowhere been successfully domesticated. Attempts have even been made to introduce the Argentine tinamou *Rhynchotus rufescens* into Britain, for they provide good sport, the young becoming independent of the parents at an early age. This also was unsuccessful. FAMILY: Tinamidae, ORDER: Tinamiformes, CLASS: Aves.   P.M.D.

TISSUES, similar cells grouped together in certain areas of the body of multicellular animals. These cells are usually specialized for a single function, thus, muscle cells contract but do not secrete, nerve cells conduct impulses but have little or no powers of contraction. The cells are held together by intercellular material such as collagen. Having become specialized for a single or at most a very narrow range of functions, they are dependent upon other parts of the organism for food, oxygen, etc. They are, therefore, associated with blood vessels, nerves and so forth. Specialization of cells in this way is an example of division of labour. Groups of tissues, each with its own functions, make up organs. See histology.

TITIS *Callicebus,* two species of monkey found in the tropical forests of South America. See New World monkeys.